Spirit Calling
KIDS

MICHAEL WUEHLER

Paperback: 978-1-966652-42-7
Hardcover: 978-1-966652-44-1
eBook: 978-1-966652-43-4
Library of Congress Control Number: 2025901833

Ordering Information:

Prime Seven Media
518 Landmann St.
Tomah City, WI 54660

Printed in the United States of America

Dedication

To my six amazing grandchildren: Grace, Amelia, Jasper, Quinn, Addy, and Alice. You were a joy and inspiration, watching you grow and mature. May God continue to bless your lives even as you blessed mine.

Papa

Table of Contents

January 1

Hello, My Precious Child! I have something wonderful to tell you: *I love you so much!* My love for you is bigger than anything you can imagine. Go ahead, stretch your arms out as wide as you can. My love is even bigger than that!

When you feel alone or need a reminder of how much I love you, remember that I sent someone very special to show you—Jesus, my Son. Jesus came to be your friend and your Savior. He's always ready to help you, especially when you make mistakes. You can ask Him for forgiveness, and He will forgive you—forever!

Want to try stretching your arms again? Forever is even bigger than that! No matter what, my love and Jesus' forgiveness are so great that they'll always surround you.

Remember: Your arms may not be big enough to reach around my love, but my love will always reach around you.

Bible Treasure:: *"For God loved the world so much that he gave his only Son so that anyone who believes in him shall not perish but have eternal life."* – John 3:16 TLB

January 2

Hello, My Dear Child! I love you so much, and as you grow, I hope you'll learn to love Me more and more. I'm here for you every day, and you can feel My love in many ways.

You can feel My love when you care for others—like your family, friends, or pets. Those warm, happy feelings when you help or comfort someone. That's a little glimpse of My love in your heart.

Talk to Me every day through prayer. Sharing your thoughts, worries, and joys with Me brings us closer, and I fill your heart with peace and happiness.

And don't forget about the Bible! When you read it, you learn about Me and see how much I care for you and everyone around you. My stories are there to help you know Me better.

As you do these things, your heart will grow in love for Me, and you'll feel My amazing love filling your life.

Remember: You can feel My love when you practice loving Me first.

Bible Treasure:: *"Love the Lord your God with all your heart, soul, and mind."* – Matthew 22:37 TLB

January 3

Hello, My Wonderful Child!

Have you ever given someone a message? Maybe you've had to tell a friend something for another friend or let your brother or sister know that dinner is ready. When you do that, you become a messenger who shares a special message!

Did you know that Jesus was My special messenger? He brought the most important message to the world: *"God loves you!"* He wanted everyone to know how much I love them.

How would you like to be My messenger, too? You can! All you have to say is, *"God loves you,"* and you share the same message Jesus did.

Let's practice together. Say it with me right now: "God loves you." Wonderful! Whenever you say those words, you spread My love and share the Good News with others.

Remember: You share God's message when you tell people you love them.

Bible Treasure: *"If that were so, then you would love me, for I have come to you from God. I am not here on my own, but he sent me."* – John 8:42 TLB

January 4

Hello, My Sweet Child!

Do you have a pet, like a puppy or a kitten? Pets need a lot of care! You feed them, keep them clean, and play with them because they love spending time with you. When you pet them, scratch their bellies, or take them for a walk, you show them they're loved and cared for.

Did you know I want you to care for others just like that? When you show love and kindness to people around you, you share my love with them.

You can show My love by caring for your family, friends, and church family. You might say, "I love you, Mommy and Daddy," or hug your brother or sister. Try it! Stretch your arms out wide and give someone a bear hug. It'll make them feel loved and make Me smile, too.

Remember: God wants us to care for and love each other.

Bible Treasure:: *Jesus repeated the question: "Simon, son of John, do you really love me?" "Yes, Lord," Peter said, "you know I am your friend." "Then take care of my sheep," Jesus said.* – John 21:16 TLB.

January 5

Hello, My Precious Child!

Did I tell you today that I love you? I do, so very much! And I've written you many love letters to remind you. You can find them all in the Bible. The Bible is filled with stories and letters, written long ago, that tell you about My love. And even though these words are old, they are just as essential for you today.

If you can't read My love letters by yourself, ask someone to read them. I know they'd be happy to! Reading one of My love letters can cheer you up when you feel sad or lonely. Imagine a big smile as you hear I love you—just like your smile right now!

Want to feel My love right now? Place your hand on your chest. Do you think that *thumpity thump* of your heartbeat? That's a reminder of My love, always there with you.

Remember: Your heartbeat is My gentle reminder that I love you.

Bible Treasure:: *"And you, dear friends in Rome, are among those he dearly loves... May all God's mercies and peace be yours."* – Romans 1:6-7 TLB.

January 6

Hello, My Little One!

How are you today? Do you remember those love letters I told you about? They're all in the Bible, and they tell beautiful stories about how much I love My children—children just like you.

One of the remarkable things I want you to know is that you can always come to Me for help. When you need Me, you can talk to Me by praying. Prayer is simply sharing what's in your heart, just like talking to a friend.

Try this whenever you want to pray: fold your hands, close your eyes, and say, *"Hear my prayer, O loving Spirit."* Just like that, you're talking to Me! I listen carefully, not only to your words but to the feelings in your heart. I know when you're happy, sad, lonely, or frustrated, and I am always here to listen.

You never have to wait for things to feel too big or hard—come to Me anytime. I am the Holy Spirit, the part of God that lives in you, and I love hearing from you.

Remember: The Holy Spirit is God's love that lives in you.

Bible Treasure: *"…He returned to heaven after giving his chosen apostles further instructions from the Holy Spirit."* – Acts 1:1-2. TLB.

January 7

Hello, My Wonderful Child!

What's the best present you've ever received? Was it a bike or maybe a pet? Imagine the excitement you felt on that special day! Over time, your pet became more than just a gift—it became something you love with all your heart. You care for it daily, feeding it, giving it water, and sharing hugs because it means so much to you.

The greatest gift anyone can give is love, and I give you My love every day. I am also giving you a gift of a very special name. I will call you My Sacred Heart. Sacred means holy or special. You are very special to Me, and our hearts always connect us. I will call you My Sacred Heart from time to time to remind you about our very special spiritual connection. Sacred Heart is also a name that will remind you how much I love you. The name Sacred Heart is My gift to you from My heart.

Remember: You have a memorable name from God, "Sacred Heart".

Bible Treasure: *"There are three things that remain— faith, hope, and love—and the greatest of these is love."* – 1 Corinthians 13:13

January 8

Good Morning, My Precious Child,

I'm so happy you're here with Me today. I love spending time with you! This week, I want to tell you about something special, prayer. Prayer is just talking to Me, like you'd talk to someone who loves you more than anything. That's Me! I'm always listening carefully to every word you say.

Remember when I said in My love letter to you, "Our Father"? That's how you can begin when you talk to Me. I'm your loving Father who cares about every part of your life. But guess what? I'm also the Holy Spirit, living inside you, filling your heart with My love, and helping you every day.

You never need fancy words or a big plan when you pray. Just start talking, and I'll be right there, listening. Tell Me about your worries, your dreams, your happy moments, and even your funny ones. Nothing is too small or too big for Me because I care about it all.

I'm never too busy for you, I am always close by.

Remember: Come to Me anytime—I can't wait to hear your voice.

Bible Treasure: *"Our Father in heaven, we honor your holy name."*—Matthew 6:9 (TLB)

January 9

Hello, My precious child.

Have you ever had a friend over to play? It's so much fun to share your toys, laugh together, and maybe even enjoy a yummy snack. Spending time with your friends is lovely— and guess what? That's how I want to spend time with you every single day. I love being part of your life.

Did you know you can invite Me to be with you and your friends too? You could read or listen to a devotional together or even make up a special prayer you share between you, your friend, and Me. I promise I'll hear every word!

When you include Me in your day, you're doing something exceptional. You're bringing My love and kindness into your life and the lives of others. When you're kind to your friends or help someone in need, you're living the way I hope you will. That's My will for you—to love, share, and include Me in everything.

I love you so much, and I am so proud of you. I will always stay close to you because you are My beloved child.

Remember: I'm with you every day.

Bible Treasure: *"May your will be done here on earth, just as it is in heaven." (Matthew 6:10 TLB)*

January 10

Hello, My dear little one.

What's your favorite food? Maybe it's macaroni and cheese, hot dogs, or tacos. Those are fun foods, but I hope you enjoy healthy things like apples, bananas, and carrots. Eating good food helps your body grow strong, with muscles and bones that can do amazing things. When you choose food that's good for you, your body becomes healthier daily.

But did you know your spirit needs food, too? Like your body, your spirit grows when you give it the proper "food." Spiritual food comes from spending time with Me. You can feed your soul by reading the Bible, praying to Me, attending church, or sharing devotions with your family.

When you enjoy this spiritual food, it helps you grow closer to Me and others who love Me, too. It makes your heart strong and full of love and kindness. I want you to succeed in body and spirit to live a life filled with joy and love.

I love watching you grow, My precious child. I'll always help you find the "food" your spirit needs.

Remember: Spiritual food helps you grow closer to Me.

Bible Treasure: *"Give us our food again today, as usual."* *(Matthew 6:11 TLB)*

January 11

Hello, My beloved child.

Has a friend ever asked you to do something you knew wasn't right? Maybe they wanted you to take something that didn't belong to you or say something mean about someone else. That feeling when you know you're being asked to do something wrong is called "temptation." It's like a little tug inside you, asking you to choose between right and wrong.

When you face temptation, I want you to remember something vital: you can always talk to Me. Stop and pray if someone ever asks you to lie or do something that doesn't feel right. Ask Me for help and guidance. I will always listen and give you the strength to make the right choice. Sometimes, I might answer you directly; others, I might send someone wise to help you.

There is nothing too big or small for you to bring to Me, My precious one. I trust you to do what is good and am always here to help you choose the right path.

Remember: Pray to Me whenever you are tempted, and I will help you.

Bible Treasure: *"Don't bring us into temptation, but deliver us from the Evil One. Amen." (Matthew 6:13 TLB)*

January 12

Hello, My precious child.

Have you ever been asked to do something you knew wasn't right? Maybe a friend wanted you to take something that didn't belong to you or say something mean about someone else. When you know you're about to make a choice, that feeling inside is called "temptation." It's like a little whisper trying to pull you toward something wrong.

When you feel tempted, remember this: you can always come to Me. I'm here for you! Pause momentarily if someone asks you to lie, cheat, or hurt others. Pray and ask Me for help. I will guide you. Sometimes, I'll give you the strength to say no; sometimes, I'll send a trusted person to help you make the right decision.

It would be best if you never faced temptation alone. I'm always by your side, ready to help you choose what is good. Trust Me to lead you because I know you want to do what's right, and I believe in you.

Remember: When you pray to Me during temptation, I will help you find the right path.

Bible Treasure: *"Don't bring us into temptation, but deliver us from the Evil One. Amen." (Matthew 6:13 TLB)*

January 13

Hello, My amazing little one.

I want you to dream big and bold dreams! Don't settle for what's easy or ordinary—reach high for the things that make your heart happy. Do you love animals? Maybe I can help you become a veterinarian to take care of puppies and kitties. Do you enjoy caring for your dolls or stuffed animals? Perhaps you'll grow up to be a doctor or nurse. Do you love talking to Me and sharing My love with others? You could become one of My ministers, helping people draw closer to Me.

This world is a whole of possibilities, and I created you to be one of a kind! Every day, I'm working in your life to help you grow into the best "you" possible. I made you unique, and there's no one else like you. You'll thrive with love, support, and encouragement from your family, teachers, and friends. And when you spend time talking and praying with Me, your spirit will grow, too.

Trust Me to do more in your life than you can ever dream or imagine. I love giving you the very best!

Remember: You can reach for the stars while standing on My shoulders.

Bible Treasure: *"Now glory be to God... able to do far more than we dare to ask or even dream of." (Ephesians 3:20 TLB)*

January 14

Hello, My Sacred Heart.

I want to invite you to talk to Me every day. That's prayer—it's simply talking to Me about anything on your heart. You can tell Me when you're happy, sad, excited, or even mad. I want to hear about your day—what you did at school, a fun game, or even a show you watched. Whatever is on your mind, I'm always listening, and whatever you tell Me is just between us unless you decide to share it.

When things aren't going well, please come to Me too. If the school feels hard, pray to Me. I can guide you to someone who can help, like your teacher or a kind friend. If you're sad, your prayers to Me can comfort your heart or even lead someone to make you smile. And when you're scared, I can fill your heart with courage and help you feel brave.

I'm always here for you, no matter what. So talk to Me anytime. I love hearing from you, My precious one.

Remember: You can always come to Me in prayer.

Bible Treasure: *"Don't worry about anything; instead, pray about everything." (Philippians 4:6 TLB)*

January 15

Hello, My Glorious Little Child,

What can I do to make your day better? Would having more toys make you happier? What if you ate candy all day or stayed in your pajamas without getting dressed—would that make your day perfect? Those things might be fun but wouldn't bring you the joy your heart longs for. That's because real happiness comes when you trust Me to care for you.

I am your Shepherd, like someone who watches over sheep in a big, green field. A shepherd ensures the sheep have everything they need—fresh grass to eat, cool water to drink, and a safe place to rest. I want to be your Shepherd, too. When you let Me guide you, I will give you everything you need to grow strong in your body and spirit.

You may not always get every toy or treat you want, but you will always have something much better—**My endless love.** Toys come and go, but My love is forever. Will you trust Me to take care of you?

Remember: I promise to lead you to a good and happy life.

Bible Treasure: *"Because the Lord is my Shepherd, I have everything I need!"* (Psalm 23:1 TLB)

January 16

Hello, My Energetic Little Child,

I see how hard you play and how much you focus each day. Sometimes, you feel tired by the end of it all, don't you? Whether you've been running around with your friends or paying close attention at school, it's natural to feel worn out after giving your best. I'm so proud of you for all the fantastic things you do. You are truly special, and if you keep working hard and staying kind, you will grow into an incredible person.

But just like your body needs rest, your soul does too. Do you know what your soul is? It's the part of Me that lives inside you, the special God-given spark that makes you who you are. When you're tired in your heart, sit with Me. Spend time listening to My words and letting them fill you with peace.

I am your Shepherd, and like sheep resting in a green field, you can find new strength when you spend time with Me. I will give your soul the rest it needs and fill your heart with My love and peace. You make Me so happy when you take time to be with Me.

Remember: I can never be far from you because I am a part of you.

Bible Treasure: "He lets me rest in the meadow grass and leads me beside the quiet streams. He gives me new strength." (Psalm 23:2-3 TLB)

January 17

Hello, My Brave Little One,

Have you ever felt afraid? Maybe it's a little scary to go down to the basement by yourself, and your imagination starts to think up things that aren't there. But when you finally go, you see there's nothing to be afraid of. Or maybe you don't want to get up to go to the bathroom at night because of the dark shadows. Have you felt like that before?

It's okay to feel afraid sometimes. I gave you fear to help keep you safe from danger, but you don't have to let it take over. I'm always with you, and I want to help. When you feel scared, you can hold My hand. Do you want to know how? Just place your hand on your heart. Do you feel the **boom, boom, boom** of your heartbeat? That's where I live, filling your heart with My love.

The next time you're afraid, touch your chest and remember I'm holding your hand. I'll guide you and keep you safe. You are never alone because I'm always close to you.

Remember: God's hand is as close as your heart.

Bible Treasure: "Even when walking through the dark valley of death I will not be afraid, for you are close beside me, guarding, guiding all the way." (Psalm 23:4 TLB)

January 18

Hello, My Kind Little One,

Do you love pizza? How about macaroni and cheese? I know those are favorites for many of My little ones. Eating delicious food is such a joy. And when you share your favorite meal with your friends. Imagine a party with friends, laughter, and tasty treats like ice cream and cake— what a fun time!

But what about the kids you don't know or maybe don't like as much? Do you think they enjoy pizza or cake as much as you do? How would it feel to invite someone like that to share a meal with you? It might feel a little scary, but also an opportunity to show love and kindness. You might even discover a new friend!

I'll be with you when you invite someone you don't know well. I'll help make the time memorable and full of My love.

Remember: I invite everyone to My table, no matter who they are. When you do the same, you show others how much I care for them, too.

Bible Treasure: "You provide delicious food for me in the presence of my enemies. You have welcomed me as your guest; blessings overflow!" (Psalm 23:5 TLB)

January 19

Hello, My Loving Little One,

Did you know that when you do something good and kind for someone, it can stay in their heart for a very long time? They might remember your kindness for years even when you forget what you did. That's why treating your friends and family with care is so important. A kind word, a helpful hand, or a smile can mean so much to someone else. But remember, the hurtful things we do can stick, too, so always choose kindness and love.

I love to bless you with good things as you grow! When I give you something good, it's called a blessing. These blessings help you become strong, happy, and full of love. My greatest blessings for you are My forgiveness, never-ending love, and promise to be with you forever. Always means! I'll never leave your side and always listen to your prayers.

So, please do your best to show kindness today, My little one.

Remember: I have made My home in your heart, and that home will last forever.

Bible Treasure: "Your goodness and unfailing kindness shall be with me all of my life, and afterwards I will live with you forever in your home." (Psalm 23:6 TLB)

January 20

Hello, My Precious Little One,

How are you today? I hope you're having a good day! But I know that sometimes My children have bad days, too. On those days, you might feel sad, lonely, or like no one understands you. But I want you to know something significant: you are never alone. I am always with you, and I will always listen to you.

When you're having a bad day, come to Me in prayer. Prayer is the special language of your heart, and I hear it loud and clear. No matter how big or small your problems feel, I want to know about them. When you pray, it's like a little lamb coming to its shepherd. I am your Shepherd, and I will gather you in My arms, listen to your worries, and comfort you.

So, remember I am here the next time you feel sad or lost. Sit quietly, talk to Me, and let My love fill your heart. I can help make even the most harrowing day better because I love you more than you can imagine.

Remember: You can always go to the shepherd as the lamb.

Bible Treasure: *"They were like sheep without a shepherd."* (Luke 9:36 TLB)

January 21

Hello, My Sacred Heart,

I love all your friends. Did you know that your friends are also My friends? I see how important they are to you. Friends are the ones you laugh and play with. They're the ones who make you feel better when you're lonely. And of course, they're the first ones you invite to your birthday party—because a party wouldn't be the same without them! Friends are a unique gift; I love watching you share joy with them.

But here's something even more astounding: you have more friends than you can imagine! Every child, every parent, and every person who loves Me is part of one big family, which makes them your friends, too. You may never meet them all, but you are connected because we share something special—**My love.**

Just like a shepherd cares for every sheep, I care for everyone on this earth. Together, we are one big family, and I am the Shepherd who brings us all together. Isn't it amazing to know you're part of something so big and full of love?

Remember: You are one sheep in a huge flock. Wow, that's a lot of friends.

Bible Treasure: *"There will be one flock with one Shepherd."* (John 10:16 TLB)

January 22

Hello, My Precious Child,

I love spending time with you. It makes Me so happy when you take the time to talk with Me and listen to My words. Did you know I'm always with you, even when you're playing, laughing, or sitting quietly? I'm proud of you for wanting to grow closer to Me.

Your family is a special gift. When you play games, share meals, or watch something together, it brings joy to everyone. I love seeing you share that happiness! You can even read this devotional with your family—your parents or siblings will see how much you learn about Me. Isn't that wonderful?

Just like food makes your body grow strong and reading helps your mind grow smart, spending time with Me helps your spirit grow, too. Every prayer, every moment in church, and every page you read brings us closer. I see how you're growing in your heart, mind, and body, and I'm so proud of you! Your parents are proud of you, too.

Keep going, My fantastic child. Keep learning, praying, and loving. Together, we'll do great things!

Remember: When you spend time with Me, you're growing into the person I've made you to be.

Bible Treasure: *"The father of a godly man has cause for joy—what pleasure a wise son is! So give your parents joy!"* (Proverbs 23:24-25)

January 23

Hello, My Precious Child,

Have you noticed how amazing it is that everyone is different? Maybe you have a friend from another country, or their parents came from far away. Isn't it fun to learn about their homeland? They might share new foods with you or teach you a few words in their language. You could even ask them how to say "pizza" in their language! Doesn't that sound exciting?

I made everyone unique, including you. No one in the whole world is exactly like you—not even twins! Your smile, your voice, your heart—I created it all to be remarkable. But even though My children are all different, there are two things they all share.

First, you all share My love. I love every single one of My children deeply and perfectly. Second, you all live together on this big, beautiful earth. It's like a giant neighborhood! Whether someone lives next door or on the other side, they're your neighbor. I want you to love them the way I love you.

You are wonderfully made and an important part of My family. Remember that always!

Remember: You are a very special person in My family.

Bible Treasure: *Distribute the land as an inheritance for yourselves and for the foreigners who live among you with their families. All children born in the land—whether or not their* **parents** *are foreigners—are to be considered citizens and have the same rights your own children have.* (Ezekiel 47:22 TLB)

January 24

Hello, My Precious Child,

I know it's no fun to be sick. Everything feels more complicated when your tummy aches or you have a fever. Your favorite foods don't taste good, and you might feel too tired to play. Sometimes, your body feels hot one minute and freezing the next. Being sick can feel frustrating, and I understand that. But I want you to know something vital: I'm with you every moment, even when you don't feel well.

Your parents love you so much and work hard to help you improve. They might bring you warm soup, take you to the doctor, or give you medicine to help you heal. While you rest, I'm working, too, allowing your body to grow strong again. It may take some time, but I'm here every step of the way. Trust Me, and let your parents care for you while I do My part.

When you feel better, I'll celebrate with you and your family! Seeing you smile and play again brings Me so much joy. You are so loved, My child, in sickness and in health.

Remember: When you are sick, I am with you and want to see you well.

Bible Treasure :*Taking her by the hand he said to her, "Get up, little girl!" (She was twelve years old.) And she jumped up and walked around! Her **parents just** couldn't get over it.* (Mark 5:41-42 TLB)

January 25

Hello, My Precious Child,

Do you know how much your parents love you? They work hard to ensure you grow up strong, smart, and kind. Sometimes, they have to do things that aren't fun, like ensuring you go to school or do your homework. But they do these things because they want what's best for you.

Learning is important! When you learn to read, you can enjoy amazing stories—like the ones in the Bible. Math helps you count, solve problems, and understand the world's workings. Everything your parents teach you now is helping you become the person I've made you to be. They follow My plan by giving you the tools you need to grow.

I hope you'll also take the time to learn about Me. Whether you go to Church School, learn from home, or pray and read about Me on your own, every little bit helps us grow closer. Prayer is a beautiful way to talk to Me, and I love hearing from you.

Your parents are doing their best, and I am with them, guiding them—and you—every step of the way.

Remember: Your parents love you, and I love you too!

Bible Treasure: *"When Jesus' parents had fulfilled all the requirements of the Law of God, they returned home to Nazareth in Galilee."* (Luke 2:39 TLB)

January 26

Hello, My Lovely Child,

You don't need to dress up or say fancy words to talk to Me. Just come as you are—I think you're amazing just the way I made you! I love hearing your prayers, whether about something big, like a school test, or something small, like thanking Me for a sunny day. I'm always here, ready to listen.

If you have a big test, don't forget to study hard. I can help you remember what you've learned and give you courage when you feel nervous. But you'll still need to do your part by practicing your spelling words and math problems. Working hard is part of growing strong and intelligent, and I'll be with you every step of the way.

Your parents are working hard, too. They love you so much and want to help you do your best. Don't forget to thank them for all they do to help you grow. We're cheering you on together because we love and want to see you shine!

Remember: I work with your parents to help you be your best.

Bible Treasure: *"After all, children don't provide for their parents. Rather, parents provide for their children."* (2 Corinthians 12:14 NLT)

January 27

Hello, My Fantastic Child,

You are such a special gift! I gave you to your parents as a blessing to fill their lives with love and joy. When you do good things at home or school, your parents' hearts are filled with pride, and their faces shine with big smiles. They love seeing you grow stronger, wiser, and kinder every day. You make Me so proud, too!

Your parents work hard to take care of you and your home. They cook, clean, and make sure you have everything you need. They also need your help! Can you tidy up your room or help with the dishes after dinner? Even a tiny "I love you" can make their day brighter. Your kindness brings joy to your home.

I need your help, too. Will you pray for your parents each night? Thank Me for them, and if you see they're feeling sad or tired, ask Me to help them. Most of all, show them love every day. When you support and love your parents, you make Me smile.

Remember: Helping your parents and showing them love pleases Me and brings joy to your family.

Bible Treasure: *"Kindness should begin at home, supporting needy parents. This pleases God very much."* (1 Timothy 5:4 TLB)

January 28

Hello, My Sacred Heart,

Did you know your parents ask for my daily help to raise you into a strong and wonderful person? They trust Me to keep you safe and guide them as they care for you. Another word for trust is "faith." Your parents have faith that I am working in your life to help you grow into the amazing person I created you to be.

By reading this devotional, your Bible, and praying, you are growing closer to Me. I love speaking to you through these words and helping you learn more about Me. Just like your body grows taller and your mind gets brighter, your spirit rises, too. This is called "spiritual growth," one of the most beautiful things to see. You may not see it with your eyes, but you can feel My love growing in your heart.

I am the peace you feel when you know everything will be okay. Your parents feel that peace, too, because they trust Me and believe in you. Have faith, My child. I'm always here to help you, and your parents are too.

Remember: I and your parents are working together to help you grow.

Bible Treasure: *"By faith, Moses' parents hid him for three months after he was born because they saw he was no ordinary child."* (Hebrews 11:23 NIV)

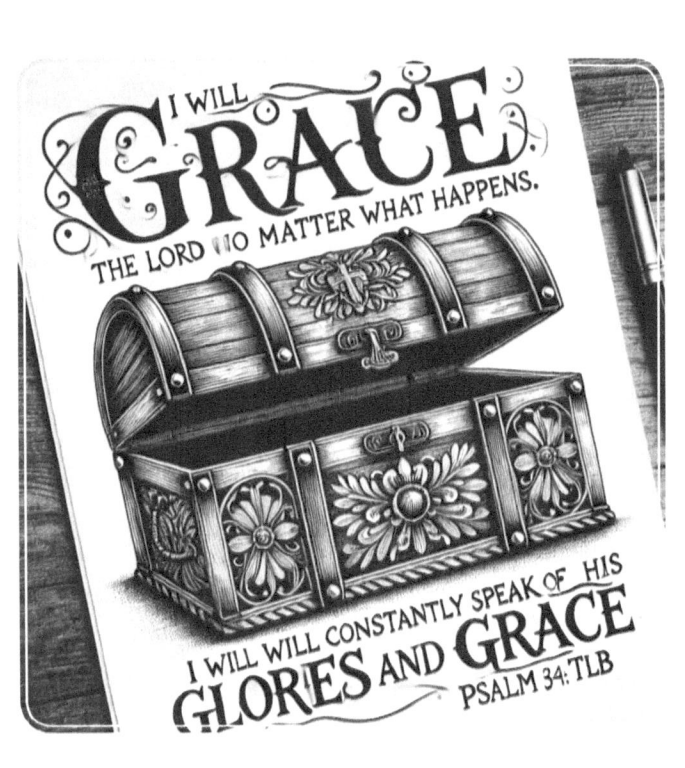

I WILL
GRACE
THE LORD NO MATTER WHAT HAPPENS.

I WILL WILL CONSTANTLY SPEAK OF HIS
GLORES AND GRACE
PSALM 34: TLB

January 29

Hello, My precious child,

Imagine walking into a toy store where you can pick any toy you like, and the cashier says, "It's free!" Maybe you'd choose a shiny bicycle, a cuddly stuffed animal, or a doll you've always wanted. Wouldn't that feel amazing? You wouldn't have to pay a single penny—what a gift!

Let Me tell you about an even better gift I give you every day. It's called grace. Grace means I give you My love, kindness, and forgiveness completely free. You don't have to earn it by being perfect or working hard. I provide you gracefully because I love you more than you can imagine.

When you make a mistake—maybe you say something unkind or do something wrong—that's called sin. Sin hurts My heart and others, but I am always ready to forgive you. All you need to do is talk to Me in prayer, tell Me you're sorry, and My grace will cover you like a warm hug. I'll wash away your sins and help you do better.

Never forget My child, My grace is always here for you. Come to Me anytime.

Remember: Grace is My free gift to you because I love you.

Bible Treasure: *"I will praise the Lord no matter what happens. I will constantly speak of His glories and grace."* (Psalm 34:1 TLB)

January 30

My dear child,

I see how hard it is to try to do what's right. You want to tidy your room, finish your homework, and be kind to your family and friends. I know you work to remember everything—like brushing your teeth and caring for yourself. I'm so proud of you for trying your best.

But sometimes, you forget or choose not to do what you're supposed to do. Maybe you didn't clean your room like your parents asked, or you didn't finish the homework your teacher gave you. When that happens, you feel bad inside, don't you? That's because you know deep down what is right.

Here's the good news: I am always here to forgive you. When you make a mistake, all you need to do is pray to Me. Tell Me you're sorry, and I'll cover you with My grace—the kind of love that forgives and helps you try again. My grace is more special than any mistake you could ever make.

So don't be afraid. I love you no matter what and am always ready to forgive.

Remember: My grace forgives you when you make mistakes.

Bible Treasure: "*The more we see our sinfulness, the more we see God's abounding grace forgiving us.*" (Romans 5:20 TLB)

January 31

Hello, My amazing child!

Can you do a handstand or ride your bike really fast? Maybe you love to swim or are super good at math or reading. I see how wonderfully talented you are! When someone is perfect at something, people say, "That child is gifted." And guess what? Those gifts and talents come from Me. I gave them to you because I love you.

But there's more! I also give special gifts called *spiritual gifts.* I give My children these abilities to help them do wonderful things for others. Maybe I gave you the gift of kindness, or perhaps you're a good listener who can help your friends when they feel sad. Every spiritual gift I give is chosen just for you to help you and others.

I was hoping you could discover the special gift I've placed inside you. My plan is to use you to share love and joy with your family, friends, and everyone you meet. So keep learning, growing, and asking Me to show you how to use your gift.

Remember, I've given you a spiritual gift to help you serve others.

Bible Treasure: *"Now you have every grace and blessing; every spiritual gift... are yours."* (1 Corinthians 1:7 TLB)

February 1

My precious child,

Do you remember how I told you about the special gifts I give to all my children? Each of you has unique abilities to help others and share My love with the world. There are many gifts because people have many needs, and I choose the right one for you. But today, I want to tell you about a gift I give *everyone*—the greatest gift.

That gift is Me! I, the Holy Spirit, live inside you. I live with your family, friends, and everyone who believes in Me. Even though people may look different on the outside, on the inside, they are the same because I live in their hearts.

You don't have to search for or wait to find Me—I'm already here! You can talk to Me anytime about anything. I'm closer to you than your hands or feet, always ready to help, comfort, and guide you.

No matter where you go or what you face, I am with you. You are never alone.

Remember: I am the Holy Spirit, God's gift to you.

Bible Treasure: *"And God has actually given us His Spirit... to tell us about the wonderful free gifts of grace."* (1 Corinthians 2:12 TLB)

February 2

Hello, My wonderful child!

Do you remember what grace means? Grace is a gift you didn't earn, but I give it to you because I love you. My grace forgives your sins when you ask, but it's even more than that. Grace is also about the blessings I pour into your life—free, loving gifts just for you.

Have you noticed My blessings? I made the sun, moon, stars, and everything on earth to make your life beautiful and complete. I placed you in a family to help you grow strong and wise. I gave you teachers, coaches, pastors, and friends to guide and cheer you on as you learn and succeed.

You have a bright mind, a strong body, and a joyful spirit—all blessings from Me. And the biggest blessing? Your very life! I created you as a unique, one-of-a-kind gift to the world. Take a moment to enjoy all the beautiful things I've given you, and remember how much I love you.

Remember: Your life and every good thing in it is a blessing from Me.

Bible Treasure: "May the grace of our Lord Jesus Christ be with you all. May God's love and the Holy Spirit's friendship be yours." (2 Corinthians 13:14 TLB)

February 4

Hello, My Sacred Heart,

When you find yourself in trouble or facing something hard, pray to me. I'm always here, ready to listen and help. Don't forget to tell your parents about what's going on. They love you and want to help, and they might even pray with you as you talk to Me. You are never alone—there are people and My presence to support you.

Sharing your troubles with Me is like letting go of a heavy load you've been carrying. My grace will lift that weight and fill your heart with peace. Grace isn't just something to know about; it's something you can feel deep inside. It's my love and forgiveness gift when you need it most.

I want you to experience the power of My grace firsthand. When you're scared, worried, or hurt, come to Me. You'll feel My love wrap around you like a warm hug, and you'll know you're never alone.

Remember: My grace is something you can feel. Enjoy it often.

Bible Treasure: *"So let us come boldly to the very throne of God... to find grace to help us in our times of need."* (Hebrews 4:16 TLB)

February 5

Hello, My dear child,

I see you trying hard to be good, even when it feels difficult. Your teacher wants you to follow the rules, your parents remind you to sit up straight, and sometimes your grandparents ask you to try food that seems strange. Even your brother or sister may not want to share their toys, and there are chores you don't always feel like doing—like walking the dog.

I understand how hard it can be. But remember this: I am always here to help you. Sin happens when you say or do things that hurt others—whether in their body, mind, or heart. When someone feels sad or hurt because of your actions, that's not what I want for you.

Don't hesitate to come to Me if you feel you've done something wrong. Ask Me for forgiveness, and I will forgive you every time. Then go to the person you've hurt and say, "I'm sorry." I'll help you make things right.

Always try to choose kindness and goodness. When you do what's right, your heart will be joyful, and I will be proud of you.

Remember, you're never alone—I'm always here.

Bible Treasure: It can be bright with joy if you will do what you should! But if you refuse to obey, watch out. **Sin** is waiting to attack you, longing to destroy you. But you can conquer it!" (Genesis 4:7 TLB)

February 6

Hello, My lovely child,

Do you know what your name means? If you don't, why not ask your parents? Maybe they chose your name because they loved how it sounded or it has a special meaning. Ask them to help you look up the definition if you're curious. It's fun to learn more about the name that makes you *you*!

Do you know what Jesus' name means? His name means "Savior." That's because He came to save everyone from their sins. When Jesus was born, it was the best gift ever—He brought the gift of forgiveness to all My children, including you.

Sometimes, you might need to correct something or do something differently. That's called sin. But don't be afraid My dear one. I will forgive you when you come to Me and ask for forgiveness in Jesus' name. You don't have to remember every mistake—ask Me to forgive all your sins, and Jesus will take care of the rest.

You are so loved, and I am always here to help you grow and do what's right.

Remember: Jesus came to be your Savior; you can always have a fresh start because of Him.

Bible Treasure: And she will have a Son, and you shall name him Jesus (meaning 'Savior'), for he will save his people from their **sin**s. (Matthew 1:2 LTB)

February 7

Hello, My dear child,

Were you baptized? Many of My precious children were baptized when they were very little, too young to remember. If you don't know, ask your parents about that special day. Maybe they even have pictures or a video of your baptism. It's a beautiful way to see how much I love you.

Baptism is a sign that your sins are forgiven. Think of it like this: when Jesus forgives you, it's as if all the wrong things you've done are washed away like dirt being rinsed off in the water. Imagine all your sins being flushed down the drain, gone forever—so far away, it's as if they never happened.

Your baptism is a reminder that you are clean in My sight, but it's also a call to try your best not to sin. Remember, even when you make mistakes, you can always come to Me, and I'll forgive you.

Remember: I am so proud of you, My beloved child. You are washed clean, loved deeply, and forever Mine.

Bible Verse To Remember: Then John went from place to place on both sides of the Jordan River, preaching that people should be baptized to show that they had turned to God and away from their **sin**s, in order to be forgiven. (Luke 3:3 TLB)

February 8

Hello, My child of God,

I see everything you do, but not because I want to know if you've been good or bad. I watch because I love you so much, and I care about every part of your life. I do notice when you make mistakes or treat someone in a way that's not kind. I want you to pay attention, too—to see when your words or actions might hurt someone else.

When you realize you've done something wrong, don't be afraid to say, "I'm sorry." Those three little words are so powerful. They help heal the hurt between you, the person you wronged, and Me. Saying "I'm sorry" shows Me that you understand what you did wasn't right and want to grow and improve.

Every time you say sorry, you're growing in your faith. You're learning to care about how your actions affect others, making Me proud.

Remember: My forgiveness is always here for you, and I'm cheering you on as you learn to love others more daily.

Bible Treasure: Seeing their faith, Jesus said to the man, "My friend, your **sin**s are forgiven!" (Luke 5:20 TLB)

February 9

Hello, My learning child.

Do you know how much I love you? I will always forgive your sins. Forgiving you is one of the ways I show My deep love for all My children. But when you sin, it can feel like a giant boulder is put between us—so big you can't see over it or find a way around it. That's why I ask you to confess your sins to Me. When you tell Me what you've done wrong, I take that giant boulder away, and we're close again.

When I forgive you, I hope it inspires others to forgive you, too. Forgiveness isn't just for you and Me—it helps everyone feel like friends again. But remember, when I forgive you, it's also a chance to learn. Each mistake can teach you how to choose better next time. Try not to keep doing the wrong thing repeatedly because that can become a bad habit, and I want so much more for you than that.

Remember: No matter what, I'll always forgive you. Keep growing, keep learning, and keep loving.

Bible Treasure: "No, sir," she said. And Jesus said, "Neither do I. Go and **sin** no more." (John 8:11 TLB)

February 10

Hello, My baptized child.

Do you remember how you received Me as a special gift? I am the Holy Spirit, and I came to you when you were baptized. Baptism is a beautiful way to show you're ready to follow Me. When you turn away from sin and live in My love, you make room for Me in your heart.

I'm here to help you learn and grow. Your Church School teachers will teach you more about Me, and your pastor will share stories and sermons to show you how I can guide you to live a good life. The Bible is another way to learn about Me and what I want for you.

When you were baptized, you were baptized in My name— the name of the Father, the Son, and the Holy Spirit. All three names are Me! I am God who creates, loves, and forgives. I'm here to help you every day, and you can come to Me in prayer anytime you need guidance or comfort.

Remember: I will always be with you, helping you grow in faith and love.

Bible Treasure: And Peter replied, "Each one of you must turn from **sin**, return to God, and be baptized in the name of Jesus Christ for the forgiveness of your **sin**s; then you also shall receive this gift, the Holy Spirit. (Act 2:38 TLB)

February 11

Hello, My Sacred Heart.

I know it can be hard not to judge others sometimes. Maybe you think someone's clothes look strange or funny or hear someone speak with an accent and feel like giggling. When you think about others this way, you're judging them, deciding they're different—and maybe even thinking you're better. But that's not how I want you to see people.

Remember, you don't know everyone's story. A person who walks funny might have a hurt leg. Someone who speaks differently might have learned another language or have trouble speaking clearly. Instead of judging them, try to love them. That's your job, My child—to love everyone as best as possible. If someone is behaving poorly or sinning, pray for them and let adults like your pastor or family leaders handle it.

When you choose to pray for someone instead of judging them, you invite Me into that moment. I'll help you understand them better, and who knows? You might even make a new friend!

Remember: Loving others instead of judging them makes your heart more like Mine.

Bible Treasure: It isn't our job to judge outsiders. It is certainly our job to judge and deal strongly with those who are members of the church and who are **sin**ning in these ways. (1 Corinthians 5:12 TLB)

February 12

Hello, My growing child,

Do you like being happy? I know you do because I created you to enjoy laughter, smiles, and joy. It makes Me glad to see you smile when you play your favorite game or feel the wind in your hair as you ride your bike. Spending time with friends and learning new things at school can make your day brighter, too. These moments of happiness are gifts from Me because I love you.

But do you know what brings the greatest joy? Spending time with Me. When you read about Me, talk to Me in prayer, or share your thoughts with Me, I fill your heart with a joy that lasts forever. I love seeing you grow closer to Me every day.

Your faith is like a tiny plant that needs care to grow strong. Reading about Me, praying, and learning more about My love for you, your faith will grow deep and unshakable— like roots in good soil. And as your faith grows, so does your joy because I pour My love into your heart.

Remember, I am always with you, helping your faith grow and filling your life with joy.

Bible Treasure: "The seed on rocky soil represents those who hear the message and receive it with joy." (Matthew 13:20 TLB)

February 13

Hello, My Precious Child,

Do you know I love sharing good news? Sometimes, I send angels to bring My messages. But most often, I choose ordinary people like you to share My love and joy with others. Isn't that amazing? You can be one of My special messengers!

Being My messenger is simple. All you have to do is tell people about My love for them. Let them know how much I care for them and how they are never alone because I am always with them. You can share Bible verses that remind them of My promises or pray with them, asking Me to listen to your hearts together. Each time you do, you'll bring joy to their lives, and I'll also fill your heart with joy.

When you tell others about Me, you spread light in their lives. You're showing them how much I love them and how they can feel My peace and happiness.

Rember: So, go ahead, My little messenger. Share My love, and watch how joy grows wherever you go!

Bible Treasure: "Don't be afraid!" the angel said. "I bring you the most joyful news ever announced, and it is for everyone!" (Luke 2:10 TLB)

February 14

Hello, My Devoted Child,

Do you know how much joy I feel when you are part of a church family? Your church is a special place where you can worship Me, learn about My love, and share happy moments with others. Whether singing songs, listening to stories about Me in Church School, or enjoying snacks with friends, every moment in your church can fill your heart with joy—and that makes Me smile.

Your church family loves you, just as I do. I hope you feel closer to Me each time you're there. I want you to pray for your church too. Your pastor works very hard to teach and guide everyone. Pray for your Church School teachers, who prepare lessons just for you so you can grow in faith and love.

Be joyful about all the beautiful things that happen in your church. Celebrate the friendships, the prayers, and the love you share with others.

Remember: Seeing you happy and growing closer to Me in church fills My heart with delight.

Bible Treasure: "They worshiped together regularly at the Temple each day, met in small groups in homes for Communion, and shared their meals with great joy and thankfulness." (Acts 2:46 TLB)

February 15

Hello, My Precious Child,

Do you remember how excited you felt when you got your favorite new toy? Or the joy bubbling when you finally learned to ride your bike? That happiness is a beautiful gift. It's the same joy I give when someone finds Me for the first time.

When someone who doesn't know Me begins to believe in Me, they become a "convert." That means they've started a brand-new journey with Me in their heart. It's like learning something fantastic and feeling proud and happy simultaneously. My presence fills them with a deep, warm joy that makes their hearts sing.

I want you to feel joy whenever you think of Me, talk to Me, or pray. Whenever you draw close to Me, I fill you with love and happiness. And guess what? When you spend time with Me, it brings Me so much joy, too!

Let My joy fill your heart, and share it with others.

Remember, My child, I'm always with you, loving and filling your life with My happiness.

Bible Treasure: "And their converts were filled with joy and with the Holy Spirit." (Acts 13:42 TLB)

February 16

Hello, My Joy filled Child,

Do you like helping others? You could wash the dishes after dinner, help clean the yard, or lend a hand to your teacher at school. When you help, you're sharing something extraordinary—My joy. Have you noticed how good it feels when someone helps you? That's Me, filling your heart with happiness through their kindness.

Every time you help someone, you're doing what I love for My children to do. You are spreading goodness and joy; those you allow can feel My love through you. When you bring others joy, you share a little piece of My Spirit with them. Isn't that amazing?

I want all My children to be helpers, spreading kindness and happiness wherever they go. When you make someone smile or feel loved, you're doing My work, and I'm so proud of you.

Remember: Keep sharing My joy—it lights up the world!

Bible Treasure: "For, after all, the important thing for us as Christians is not what we eat or drink but stirring up goodness and peace and joy from the Holy Spirit." (Romans 14:17 TLB)

February 17

Hello, My Sacred Heart,

I am here with you, closer than the air you breathe. I never leave you—not for a moment. My presence is a gift, and I bring you something extraordinary called spiritual fruit. It's not like apples or oranges growing on a tree, but something unique that grows in your heart.

One of the fruits I plant in you is joy. Joy fills you with happiness that bubbles up like laughter and shines like a bright smile. When you laugh, sing, or play, you are letting My joy grow inside you—which makes Me so happy! Your happiness brings Me joy, too.

But did you know you can share this fruit with others? When you do something kind, say something encouraging, or make someone laugh, you also plant joy in their hearts. I love to see that my children fill the world with happiness.

So, sing your happy songs, laugh loudly, and play with a big smile.

Remember: These happy moments are My gift to you, My beautiful child.

Bible Treasure: "But when the Holy Spirit controls our lives, he will produce this kind of fruit in us: love, joy, peace, patience, kindness, goodness, faithfulness." (Galatians 5:22 NIV)

February 19

Beloved child,

Did you know that the same thing that happened to Jesus can happen to you? Jesus went to the Jorden River to be baptized by John the Baptist. As he was coming up out of the waters, I descended on him in the form of a dove. I came down from heaven to be a part of Jesus' life here. I came to Jesus as a dove to show everyone watching that the peace of God was coming into Jesus at his baptism.

When a pastor baptizes people, sometimes there is a picture of a dove somewhere in the church. The dove's image reminds everyone that I come to be with them in their baptism.

Baptism shows everyone that I am in their lives. You are baptized with water, just like Jesus. I come down from heaven to live in you, just as I did with Jesus.

Remember, you are loved, and you are mine forever.

Bible Verse To Rember: After his **baptism**, as soon as Jesus came up out of the water, the heavens were opened to him and he saw the Spirit of God coming down in the form of a dove. (Matthew 3:16 GNT)

February 20

You Are Part of My Family Dear Child,

Did you know your baptism makes you part of a huge family? That family is called "Christian," and it's made up of people worldwide who follow Jesus. When you're baptized, I, the Holy Spirit, come into your life, just like I did with Jesus. That's when you become part of God's family forever!

Every Christian is baptized, but sometimes in different ways. Some are gently dipped under water. Others have water sprinkled on their heads or poured over them. The method doesn't matter—what matters is that baptism shows you belong to Jesus. It's a way of saying, "Yes! I want to follow Him!"

When you are baptized, I begin working in your heart and life, helping you follow Jesus' teachings and grow in love, kindness, and faith. You are never alone because I am always with you. And just like every family member is essential, so are you.

Remember, being part of God's family means being loved, treasured, and called to live like Jesus. Hold onto this truth: *You belong.*

Bible Verse To Remember: "Oh, yes," they said, "we are!" And Jesus said, "You shall indeed drink from my cup and be baptized with my **baptism**, (Matthew 10:39 GNT)

February 21

Hello, My Gifted Child,

Did you know there are different ways people are baptized? Some are gently dunked in water, others pour water over their heads, and some are sprinkled with water. You might know someone who was baptized differently than you. But let me tell you a secret: there's no "better" way to be baptized.

I come to My children no matter how they choose to be baptized. What matters is that you receive baptism because it's My promise to come and live in your heart. Your church follows a way of baptizing that it believes is best, and I am with you every step of the way.

When you are baptized, I fill your life with joy, love, and My presence. Baptism signifies that you want to follow Jesus and live the way He teaches. That's what's important—not the method, but the promise. I was so pleased when you were baptized!

Remember, baptism is a beautiful gift that forever makes you part of God's family. I will always be with you.

Bible Verse To Remember: "One day someone began an argument with John's disciples, telling them that Jesus' baptism was best." (John 3:25 GNT)

February 22

Holy My Glorious Child,

Do you know what makes baptism so unique? No matter how it's done—whether you're dipped in water, sprinkled, or have water poured over you—it's all the same baptism Jesus brought.

When John the Baptist baptized people, he told them to turn from their evil ways. His baptism helped people prepare their hearts for Jesus. But when Jesus came, He brought something even more significant. Jesus' baptism shows your repentance and fills you with My presence. When you are baptized, I, the Holy Spirit, come to you as a gift!

It doesn't matter where you live or how your church practices baptism. A child in Africa, a child in Asia, and a child right where you are—all receive the same beautiful gift of My love and guidance. We may look different or speak different languages, but we all share the same Lord, faith, and baptism.

Remember, baptism is a way to say, "Yes, I belong to Jesus!" And when you do, I will always be with you, filling your life with love, joy, and peace.

Bible Verse: "For us there is only one Lord, one faith, one baptism." (Ephesians 4:5 GNT)

February 23

My Sacred Heart,

Did you know I love talking to you? I spoke to the people during Jesus' time, too. At Jesus' baptism, I spoke so everyone would know that Jesus and I are one. Jesus was part of Me, and I was part of Him. That's because Jesus was God alive on earth.

Jesus was God and human—just like you in some ways! He felt joy, sadness, and even hurt like you do. But He was also God, showing everyone how much I love them and want to be close to them.

At Jesus' baptism, I spoke from heaven so people would know He was My Son. And guess what? Just like I was with Jesus, I am with you too! I live in you, guiding, comforting, and reminding you how much you are loved.

Remember, Jesus understands you because He lived a human life. And because I live in you, you are never alone—just like Jesus was never alone.

Bible Verse: "And we know He is, because God said so with a voice from heaven when Jesus was baptized." (1 John 5:6-8 GNT)

February 24

Hi, It's Me—Your Closest Friend!

Do you go to church and receive Communion? Maybe your church waits until you've been baptized or confirmed before you take part in this special moment. Whenever it happens, Communion isn't just any meal—it's a chance to remember something amazing about Jesus!

Let me take you back to a very special dinner Jesus had with His closest friends. Picture it: a cozy room, a table full of food, and Jesus sitting with His disciples, smiling and talking. During the meal, Jesus picked up some bread. He looked around the table and said, **"This bread is like my body. When you eat it, remember me."** Then, later in the meal, He held up a cup of wine and said, **"This wine is like my blood. When you drink it, remember me."**

What Jesus was telling them—and you—is that this meal is more than just food. It's about love, sacrifice, and staying connected to Him. Every time you share Communion, you're invited to remember how much Jesus loves you and how He gave everything to save you.

Remember: Holy Communion is a meal Jesus invites you to share, so you can remember Him and feel His love.

Bible Verse: As they were eating, Jesus took a small loaf of bread and blessed it and broke it apart and gave it to the disciples and said, "Take it and eat it, for this is my body." [27] And he took a cup of wine and gave thanks for it and gave it to them and said, "Each one drink from it, [28] for this is my blood, sealing the new covenant. It is poured out to forgive the sins of multitudes. (Matthew 26:26-27 TLB)

February 25

Hi, It's Me, how are you, My glorious child?

Have you ever had to say goodbye to a good friend? Maybe they moved to a new town or switched schools. I know how much that can hurt. Losing someone you care about takes work. Did you know Jesus understands that feeling too? One of His closest friends betrayed Him, which made His heart so heavy.

But here's some good news: when you feel far from a friend, Jesus can help bring you closer. That's part of the gift of Communion! When you take the bread and juice, Jesus invites you to remember Him—but you can also think about your friend. Communion isn't just about you and Jesus; we are connected as one big family.

Whenever you take Communion, I'm right there with you, helping you feel united with Jesus and the people you love—even if they're far away. Jesus' love is like a bridge, tying hearts together. So, as you take Communion, let Jesus remind you that you, your friend, and everyone who follows Him are united in His love.

Remember: Through Communion, Jesus connects us all—no matter where we are.

Bible Verse: That evening as he sat eating with the Twelve, he said, "One of you will betray me." (Matthew 26:20-21 TLB)

February 26

Hi, My blessed child!

Did you know the bread you eat at Communion has a very special meaning? Let me tell you a story about the first time it was shared.

A long time ago, Jesus sat at a table with His closest friends, the disciples. They were celebrating a memorable holiday together. During the meal, Jesus picked up a piece of bread, held it, and blessed it. Then He said, **"This bread is like my body. Whenever you eat it, remember me."**

That bread became more than just food—a way to feel close to Jesus. Every time His friends ate it, they remembered His love and all the amazing things He did for them.

When you go up for Communion, I'll be right there with you, whispering in your heart. I'll help you see that the bread isn't just bread—a reminder of Jesus, His love, and His life. So, when you eat it, think about Him and celebrate His gift.

Remember: The bread of Communion reminds you of Jesus' love and His presence with you.

Bible Verse: As they were eating, Jesus took a small loaf of bread and blessed it and broke it apart and gave it to the disciples and said, "Take it and eat it, for this is my body. (Matthew 26:26 TLB)

February 27

Hi, It's Me—your life guide!

Hi there, my child! Have you ever wondered about the little cup you drink from during Communion? Whether filled with wine or grape juice, it's more than just a drink—it's a powerful reminder of Jesus' love for you!

Let me take you back to Jesus' special meal with His friends, the disciples. He picked up a cup of wine and said, **"This is like my blood. Whenever you drink it, remember me."** I know that might sound a little strange, but here's what it means: Jesus gave His life so you could be free from sin and come close to Me anytime—through prayer, love, and life.

When you sip from that cup during Communion, it's not just about the juice or wine but remembering the incredible gift Jesus gave. He loves you so much that He made a way for you to stay connected to Him and to Me always.

So next time you drink from the little cup, I'll be there with you, reminding your heart how much Jesus loves you. Together, we'll celebrate the extraordinary life He gave for you!

Remember: The cup reminds you of Jesus' incredible love and the life He gave so you could be close to Him.

Bible Verse: And he took a cup of wine and gave thanks for it and gave it to them and said, "Each one drink from it, [28] for this is my blood, sealing the new covenant. It is poured out to forgive the sins of multitudes. (Matthew 26:27 TLB)

February 28

Hey there, my child!

Let Me tell you a story about a special night—the night Jesus gave us the first Communion. He was celebrating Passover with His disciples; it was no ordinary meal.

A long time ago, in Egypt, God's people were slaves. But God had a rescue plan! He sent an angel to free them. The people of Israel marked their doors with the blood of a lamb, and when the angel saw the mark, it would Pass Over their houses, keeping them safe. That's why it's called Passover!

It gets even more impressive now that Jesus became like that lamb for you. He gave His life so you could be free— not from Egypt, but from sin. When you accept Jesus as your Savior, you can live a life whole of love, peace, and hope.

Every time you take Communion, you're remembering this incredible gift! When you eat the bread and drink from the cup, you're celebrating how much Jesus loves you and how He saves you. I'll be right there, helping you feel His love.

Remember, Communion started at a Passover meal and celebrates the freedom Jesus gives you!

Bible Verse: and he said, "I have looked forward to this hour with deep longing, anxious to eat this **Passover meal** with you before my suffering begins. (Luke 22:15 TLB)

March 1

Hi, my lovely child!

Do you know what makes Communion so special? It's not just about the bread or the cup—it's about love. On the night Jesus shared the first Communion with His disciples, He gave them an important commandment: **"Love one another as I have loved you."**

And guess what? I want you to know I love you just as much as Jesus loves you! You are so precious to Me, and My love for you is more significant than you can imagine. But here's the best part—you can help Me share that love with others!

Every time you're kind to your parents, share with your siblings, help a friend, or even smile at someone who's feeling sad, you're sharing My love. It's like sprinkling kindness everywhere you go! When you treat people the way Jesus would, you show them how much they matter to Me.

So, My blessed child, will you help Me spread love today? Let's work together to make the world brighter with Jesus' love.

Remember: Jesus gave us a commandment to love one another. Let's share His love every day!

Bible Verse: "And so I am giving a new commandment to you now—love each other just as much as I love you. [35] Your strong love for each other will prove to the world that you are my disciples." (John 13:34 TLB)

March 2

Hi, My Sacred Heart!

Did you know that when you take Communion, you become part of a giant, fantastic family stretching worldwide? It's true!

Imagine this: when you take the bread, a young boy in Australia is doing the same thing. When you sip from the Communion cup, a girl in China might be sipping too. A grandmother in Japan, a man in Argentina, or a child in Africa are all part of your family. Isn't that incredible? Communion connects you to people everywhere!

When you share in this holy meal, you're remembering Jesus and joining your brothers and sisters worldwide in celebrating His love. Communion reminds us that we're all united in Me, no matter where we live or what language we speak.

Next time you take Communion, imagine the whole world at one big table with Me at the center. It's one of My favorite moments because it shows how connected we are.

Remember: When you take Communion, you're sharing it with My children around the earth. And I love seeing My family united!

When we ask the Lord's blessing upon our drinking from the cup of wine at the Lord's Table, this means, doesn't it, that all who drink it are sharing together the blessing of Christ's blood? And when we break off pieces of the bread from the loaf to eat there together, this shows that we are sharing together in the benefits of his body. (1 Corinthians 10:16 TLB)

"ABRAHAM THOW AMSELF IN THE LORD, HE WE WAS LAUHGHING IN BELIEF! GENESSIS 17:17, TLB

March 3

Hello, My precious child!

People have been worshiping Me for a very long time—even before churches or hymns. Worship is when you stop, focus on Me, and show your love. When you're in church, singing songs, reading the Bible, or praying, you're honoring Me. I love seeing My children come together to worship!

But here's a secret: you don't need a building to worship Me. Abraham didn't have a church or choir but still worshiped Me. Once, I promised him he'd have a baby even though he was 100 years old and Sarah was 90! He laughed in disbelief but trusted Me, and his worship mattered.

You can worship Me anytime—sing, pray, or think about My love for you. Wherever you are, I'm there, too. I notice every little moment you spend with Me, and I treasure it.

Remember: Worship isn't about where you are but your heart.

Bible Treasure: *"Abraham threw himself down in worship before the Lord, but inside he was laughing in disbelief!" (Genesis 17:17, TLB)*

March 4

Hello, My beautiful child!

Do you ever feel a warm glow deep inside you? That's your spirit reaching out to me and wanting to connect. I'm always here, ready to make our bond stronger. Worship is one of the most extraordinary ways we can grow closer.

A long time ago, wise men—Magi from faraway lands—felt that same warmth in their hearts when Jesus was born. They knew something extraordinary had happened. They followed a star and traveled a great distance to worship Him. Their journey was long, but their hearts were full of joy.

You don't have to travel far to worship Me. When you go to church, sing songs, pray, and hear stories about Me, your spirit feels alive—just like the Magi felt! Worshiping Me with your friends and family makes your connection to Me even stronger, and I love it when you do.

So, when you feel that warm glow inside, know that it's your spirit calling out to Me. Let's grow closer together—through worship, love, and joy!

Remember: When you worship with others, your spirit grows closer to Me.

Bible Treasure: *"Where is the newborn King of the Jews? For we have seen his star and have come to worship Him."* *(Matthew 2:2 TLB)*

March 5

Hi, My wonderful child!

Did you know that Jesus loved to worship, too? He would gather with His friends and followers at the synagogue— their version of church. They read from the Bible, sang hymns from the Book of Psalms, and listened to Jesus share messages about Me. Worship brought them closer to each other and Me, and it helped them grow in love and faith.

When you go to church, you're following Jesus' example! You sing, pray, and listen to stories from the Bible just like He did. I love watching you worship with your friends and family. Every hymn you sing, and every prayer you whisper makes My heart so happy.

But here's something special to remember: worship doesn't only happen in church. You can talk to Me or pray anytime, anywhere. Whether you're at home, outside, or with friends, I'm always listening. Just like Jesus found time to worship, you can find time each day to spend with Me. And guess what? I take time every moment to be with you, too.

Remember: Jesus made time to worship, and you can too!

Bible Treasure: *"Jesus and His companions went into the synagogue, where He preached." (Mark 1:21 TLB)*

March 6

Hello, My joyful child!

Worshiping Me should be fun and exciting! I want you to laugh, sing, and feel the happiness in your heart when you spend time with Me. Clap your hands, stomp your feet, and let your voice ring out with songs about My glory. It makes Me so happy when I see the big, beautiful smile on your soul as you worship!

When you come to worship, I want you to know I'm with you. My mercy and love surround you like a warm hug. You might not see them, but you can feel them. Mercy is My special gift to you—a gift of salvation that comes because I love you so much.

Every time you step into church, I'm waiting to welcome you with open arms. I can't wait to share My joy with you. Worship is our time to be together, laugh, sing, and feel the happiness I have when I'm with you.

Remember: Worship is a time to feel the joy of being with Me.

Bible Treasure: *"But as for me, I will come into your Temple protected by your mercy and your love; I will worship you with deepest awe." (Psalm 5:7 TLB)*

March 7

Hi, My precious child!

Did you know the church is a special place where people who believe in Me gather to worship? It's a place where you can sing songs about Me, hear stories from My Word, and learn how to pray just like My people did in the Bible. Being part of a church helps you grow in your faith and understand who I am.

But here's something wonderful: you don't have to be at church to worship Me. Right now, as you read this at home, you're worshiping and learning more about Me. You can talk to your parents or siblings about Me, read Bible stories, or say prayers together. There are so many ways to make your house a home where I'm welcome.

I'm always here for you, no matter where you are. Start your day by reading something about Me, and end it by talking to Me in prayer. When you do, your heart becomes a little more like home to Me, too.

Remember: You can worship Me at church or at home—I'm always with you.

Bible Treasure: *"They worshiped together regularly at the Temple, met in small groups at home, and shared their meals with great joy and thankfulness." (Acts 2:46 TLB)*

March 8

Hello, My sweet child!

Do you know how much I love to hear you sing to Me? Your voice is unique, and when you worship, it fills My heart with joy. Now, imagine something amazing: everyone on earth singing together to Me—the same beautiful song at the same time. What a glorious sound that would be!

Picture it: children in the Arctic singing with children in the rainforest. People in the Gobi Desert join voices with those in the Canadian Rockies. Everyone from every corner of the world sings My sacred songs in worship. Can you hear it in your heart? It would be the most joyful music ever made.

You, My child, are part of this fantastic dream. Every time you worship, you're joining people from all over the world who sing, pray, and praise Me. Start by learning My sacred songs and singing them with all your heart. You add your voice to a beautiful, worldwide choir when you do.

Remember: When you worship, you're joining voices with people from all over the world.

Bible Treasure: *"All the earth shall worship You and sing of Your glories." (Psalm 66:4 LTB)*

March 9

Hello, My Sacred Heart!

Have you ever wondered what heaven is like? Let Me tell you a little secret: Heaven is filled with the sound of worship! It's a sacred, holy place where everyone is so happy because they are with Me, singing songs and praising Me all day. In heaven, there's no crying, no sadness, and no tears—only joy, love, and worship.

When you're in heaven, you won't need books or stories about Me because you'll see Me face to face! Doesn't that sound exciting? Heaven is where My children live in My glory and feel My love forever. Everyone there has found their greatest joy—knowing, loving, and being close to Me.

But don't worry about heaven right now, My little one. You have plenty of time to enjoy life here! Just know that a fantastic place is waiting for you. Until then, worshiping Me brings a little piece of heaven to your heart because that's when you feel closest to Me.

Remember: We are closest to heaven when we worship God.

Bible Treasure: *"Then the twenty-four Elders and four Living Beings fell down and worshiped God, saying, 'Amen! Hallelujah! Praise the Lord!'" (Revelation 19:4 TLB)*

March 10

Hi there, My friend!

I want you to know something amazing—I'm always here for you. You can talk to Me anytime about anything. Sharing your worries or telling Me about your day makes Me so happy because I love being close to you. And guess what? When you pray, I'll listen, ready to help you feel better.

I love celebrating with you, too! Birthdays? I'll help you make them extra joyful. Christmas? I'll sing along with you and share the excitement of unwrapping presents. Every happy moment becomes brighter when we share it.

And here's My promise: I'll never leave you. Not ever. No matter what, I'll always be your friend, cheering you on and helping you through every adventure life brings. Just say, "Come, Holy Spirit," and I'll be by your side, ready to fill your heart with love and joy.

Being your friend is My favorite thing in the world. Let's make every day unforgettable—together.

Remember: God wants to be your best friend forever.

Bible treasure: *"Yes, in my early years, when the friendship of God was felt in my home;"* (Job 29:4 TLB)

March 11

Thank you for being My friend. I have a lot of friends your age. Every one of them is just as delightful and unique as you are, My child. I enjoy hearing the sound of your voice when you pray to Me. I love it when you giggle and laugh and have fun playing **Hi there, My precious friend!**

Do you know how much I love spending time with you? Every moment of your day, whether you're playing, learning, or just being still, makes My heart happy. I'm always here, ready to listen to anything you want to share—even your biggest secrets. And guess what? I'll never tell anyone what you tell Me. Your secrets are safe with Me!

But I have a secret, too, that I hope you'll share. I love every single one of My children on this earth. That might not seem like a big secret, but some of My children don't know how much I love them yet. If you want, you can tell your friends about Me. Let them know I'd love to be their friend, too. Sharing My love is a secret I'm happy for you to spread!

So, My dear, let's make this our special mission: to bring more friends into our special spiritual relationship.

Remember: Go is friends to everyone.

Remember: *"Friendship with God is reserved for those who reverence him. With them alone he shares the secrets of his promises."* (Psalm 25:14 TLB)

March 12

Hello, My precious friend!

I love seeing how you care for the people around you. Did you know that honesty and kindness are some of the best gifts you can give your friends? Lies are tricky—they can tangle you up in ways you don't expect. One lie can lead to another, and soon, it's hard to keep track. But when you choose honesty, your heart feels light, and your friendships grow stronger.

Here's a little secret: the best way to treat others is how you'd like them to treat you. Do you want kindness? Show kindness. Do you want honesty? Be truthful. Your friends count on you to be honest with them; they love you just as you are. And guess what? So do I! You don't have to make up stories or pretend to be someone else to earn My love. I already love you more than you can imagine.

Remember: Think of your friends as precious gifts from me, who are here to make life brighter. And remember, true friendships can last forever—even in heaven.

Bible Treasure: *"But shall I tell you to act that way, to buy friendship through cheating? Will this ensure your entry into an everlasting home in heaven?"* (Luke 16:9 TLB)

March 13

Hi, My wonderful friend!

Did you know that Jesus came to this earth to be everyone's friend? He wanted people to see how much I love them—how much I love *you*! Friends listen to each other, don't they? That's why Jesus made so many friends—He wanted everyone to hear about My love. When you make friends with Jesus, you make friends with Me, too, because We are one.

I hope you read about Jesus in the Bible or a storybook. You'll see how He loves to talk about Me. Jesus showed people I am the Holy Spirit, the part of God living inside you. That means I'm always with you, your forever friend, cheering you on and loving you every moment.

So, grab your Bible or favorite storybook about Jesus and discover how much I care for all My precious children.

Remember, My love for you never changes—you are My friend for life!

Bible Treasure: *"God will surely do this for you, for he always does just what he says, and he is the one who invited you into this wonderful friendship with his Son, even Christ our Lord."* (1 Corinthians 1:19 TLB)

March 14

Hello, My precious friend!

I want to help you make good choices about the people around you. Some of My children don't always behave the way they should. They might do things that hurt others or ask you to do something wrong. If that happens, be brave! Say, "No, I'm not doing that." True friends never try to get you in trouble or tell lies about others. And I want you to be that kind of true friend, too.

Stand up for what's right when you hear someone saying unkind or untrue things. Gently remind them that being honest and kind is always better. And remember, I am always with you, giving you strength and helping you make good choices.

The best friendships are built on kindness and truth. When you live this way, your friends will see My love shining through you.

Remember: You are My unique child, and I am so proud of you for choosing what is right!

Bible Treasure: *"They are the kind who craftily sneak into other people's homes and make friendships with silly, sin-burdened women and teach them their new doctrines."* (2 Timothy 3:6 TLB)

March 15

Hello, My amazing friend!

Did I mention how much I love being your friend? I'm with you in everything you do—whether you're running, playing, or just being your silly, joyful self. I love watching you have fun! Your laughter makes Me so happy, and I feel your joy when life is going wonderfully.

But guess what? I'm not just your friend during the good times. When life feels hard or you're sad, I'm still here. Come to Me in prayer and tell Me what's on your heart. Sharing your worries with Me will help lighten your load. That's what best friends do—they listen and help.

I also love hearing about your victories! Did you do well in school or sports? Please share it with Me! When you practice sharing the happy things, it makes sharing the hard stuff even easier.

Remember: No matter what, I'm always here for you, cheering you on and filling your heart with My love.

Bible Treasure: *"May the grace of our Lord Jesus Christ be with you all. May God's love and the Holy Spirit's friendship be yours."* (2 Corinthians 13:14 TLB)

March 16

Hi, My Sacred Heart!

Friends make life so much brighter, don't they? I hope you find terrific friends no matter where you live. Do you know one of the best places to meet new friends? The church! It's a place full of people who love Me like you do.

Visiting a church is a great way to feel at home if you ever move to a new town. You might hear songs and hymns you already know and love. Many churches even have classes or groups just for kids your age where you can learn more about Me, ask questions, and make friends who share your love for God.

I never want you to feel lonely, My precious child. That's one reason I created the church—so you'd always have a place to belong, where you're loved and surrounded by people who care about you.

Remember: Wherever life takes you, My church family welcomes you with open arms.

Bible Treasure: *"They have told the church here of your friendship and your loving deeds. I am glad when you send them on their way with a generous gift."* (3 John 1:3 TLB)

March 17

Hi, My Amazing Child!

It's Me, your spiritual teacher, and I'm so excited to spend time with you! I love having these moments together because you are so special to Me. Learning about Me is never meant to be tedious or complicated. Think of it as an adventure where I show you incredible things about who I am and who I created you to be. Doesn't that sound fun?

You've got parents, teachers, and friends who help you grow, but the time we share here is just for you and Me. When you take time to be with Me daily, it's like practicing for something extraordinary—like becoming the person I made you to be. The more you practice, the stronger and happier your spirit will grow.

I want you to know something important: I love it when you're joyful! Share every smile, laugh, and happy moment with Me. I celebrate your happiness because I love you so much.

Someday, you'll outgrow this book, and that's okay. It means you're growing in faith, and that's precisely what I hope for you.

Remember: Let's keep growing together, one joyful day at a time.

Bible Treasure: "A wise teacher makes learning a joy." (Proverbs 15:2 TLB)

March 18

Hello, My precious one!

I've given you a brain like a treasure chest waiting to be filled with fantastic knowledge. Imagine the adventures you'll go on as you learn! You could be a doctor, saving lives; a mechanic, fixing roaring engines; or a teacher, sharing My love with others. Learning is your superpower, and I'm cheering you on every step of the way.

But you'll learn one lesson more potent than anything else: Love. That's right! Loving others—truly loving—is the most important thing you'll ever do. You see, if you learn everything about the stars and science or speak every language in the world but don't have love, it's like a loud, clanging noise. Love makes your words and actions shine with My light!

So, as you learn and grow, remember to sprinkle love everywhere. Help a needy friend, listen to someone lonely, and always show kindness. When you do, you're sharing My passion, and that's the greatest gift of all.

Remember: Loving people is the most important thing you will ever learn.

Bible Treasure: "Love others as much as I love you!" (John 15:12 TLB)

March 19

Hi, My Beloved Child!

It's Me, your Holy Guide, and I have something extraordinary to tell you: You are My precious child, and I love you more than you can imagine! When you wake up in the morning, remember this: You belong to Me, and everything you do today shows the world who I am.

When you're kind to your teachers, patient with your classmates, or helpful at home, you're reflecting My love. People will see how you act and think, *"Wow, there's something special about them!"* That's because you are filled with My love, which shines through you.

I know it's not always easy. Sometimes, your friends or family might hurt your feelings or anger you. It's tempting to yell or say something mean back. But that only makes things worse. Instead, pause. Take a deep breath. Let My love fill your heart. Forgive them, just like I forgive you every single time.

You can do it because I'm with you. Let's show the world how good and kind My children can be together. Live in a way that makes others think of Me.

Remember: Always behave like Jesus did.

Bible Treasure: Live in a way to please and honor Me, always doing good and kind things for others." (Colossians 1:10 TLB)

March 20

Hi there, My Amazing Child!

I have something exciting to share. Did you know that doing is one of the best ways to learn? You learn how to be suitable by practicing good things every day.

Think about this: When you help your parents by cleaning your room, washing dishes, or taking out the trash, you do something good. You show love and care when you help your little brother or sister by reading to them or showing them how to do something. Every time you practice kindness, you grow more assertive in doing good—just like athletes who practice to improve at their sport.

It might feel hard at first, but doing good becomes natural with practice—like skating, singing, or hitting a baseball. When you do good things, people around you see Me in you. They see My love shining through your actions, which makes My heart so happy!

Remember: Each kind act brings you closer to God and others.

Bible Treasure: You are living a new kind of life, learning more of what is right and becoming more like Christ." (Colossians 3:10 TLB)

March 21

Hi, My Precious Child!

I'm so happy you're growing and learning about Me! Church is such a wonderful place to get to know Me better. Your teachers there are excited to help you understand how to pray, read the Bible, and grow in faith. And guess what? You're not alone—your friends are learning alongside you, making it even more fun!

Don't ever be afraid to learn new things. Everyone has to start somewhere—even your parents, teachers, and pastor! One of the most beautiful lessons I want you to know is giving cheerfully. When you help someone, share your talents, or give an offering at church, it's a way to show My love. Giving isn't just about money—it's about your time, kindness, and love for others.

Here's a secret: When you give with a happy heart, it feels fantastic inside. It's one of the best ways to grow closer to Me and show the world what My love looks like.

Remember: Learning to give cheerfully is an excellent lesson in life.

Bible Treasure: "Be leaders in the spirit of cheerful giving." (2 Corinthians 8:7 TLB)

March 22

Hi Again, My Dear Child!

I want you to know something beautiful: when you do good things, you honor Me and learn to love others just like I do. Everything good I do comes from My deep love for all My children—including you! I love helping and caring for My precious ones, and I want you to do the same.

But here's something important: Stay far away from doing bad things. Bad habits are like sticky traps—they're hard to escape once you get caught in them. Instead, make *good* habits, like showing kindness and love every day. These are habits you'll never need to change. One of the best habits is learning to love people how I love them.

When you trust Me, I'll help you see who needs your kindness. Maybe it's a classmate who feels left out or a sibling who needs extra patience. Love is the greatest gift you can give, and I promise it's always worth sharing.

Remember: Love is your greatest gift; learn to share it often.

Bible Treasure: "Run from all evil things. Do what is right, trust Me, love others, and be gentle." (1 Timothy 6:11 TLB)

March 23

Hi, My Wonderful Child!

I am here for you again. I know it's not always easy to be good and follow Me every day, but I believe in you! Just like you eat healthy food to strengthen your body and go to school to improve your brain, practicing good things every day will also make your soul strong.

Think about how well you ride your bike or scooter now. You've practiced so much that it feels easy, right? But if you stop riding for years, you might forget and have to relearn. That's how it is with doing good! The more you practice being kind, forgiving, and loving, the easier it will become. Living like Me takes daily practice, but it's worth it!

What you learn and do now will stay with you as you grow up. So, practice being the best version of yourself today! Stay away from people who pull you into bad choices, and keep your heart focused on Me. I'll always guide you.

Remember. Always do your best, and you will have a great life.

Bible Treasure: "Always do your best, and you will have a great life." (Inspired by 2 Peter 2:20 TLB)

March 24

Hi, My Sacred Heart!

I want to help you build something incredible: your spirit! Just like running and playing strengthen your body and reading books develop your mind, there are unique ways to improve your spirit. Attending church, learning about Me in your classes, and reading books like this all help your faith grow.

But do you know the best way to build your spirit? It's through prayer! When you pray, it's like opening a secret, direct line between us. Your prayers tell Me what's on your heart—your joys, worries, and even the things you don't know how to say. And when you pray, I'll fill you with My strength and power to face anything that comes your way.

The more you talk to Me, the stronger your spirit becomes. I'll be right here, always listening and always ready to help. So, let's keep building your faith together—one prayer at a time!

Remember: Believing in God is the foundation for all of your life.

Bible Treasure: "Build up your life on the foundation of faith, praying in the power of the Holy Spirit." (Jude 1:20 TLB)

March 25

Hi, My Amazing Rock!

Let's start a new week and topic; I want you to know something incredible—you are strong, just like Peter! When Jesus called Peter "a stone," he said that Peter's faith was strong enough to build His church on. Guess what? I see that same potential in you. Your faith, no matter how small it feels right now, can grow into something powerful and unshakable.

Think about how rocks make a strong foundation for buildings. Without that foundation, the building could fall. Your faith is like that rock! The more you trust Me, pray to Me, and learn about Me, the stronger your foundation will become.

Even when hard times come—when you're scared, upset, or don't know what to do—remember that with Me, you're unshakable. Let's work together to strengthen your faith like a rock, My child. I'm always here, cheering you on and giving you strength!

Remember: You are the rock of your church.

Bible Treasure: You are Peter, a stone; and upon this rock I will build my church; and all the powers of hell shall not prevail against it." (Matthew 16:18 TLB)

March 26

Hello, My Precious Child,

I'm here to tell you something amazing—I'm with you daily! When life feels hard, or you're sad, I'm wrapping you in My comfort. I bring you peace, like a warm hug, and help you see that you are never alone. You can always call on Me, and I will always answer. I love you so much, and My love never changes!

Do you know how special it is to be part of a church? It's like being in a big family where everyone believes in and loves Me. Together, you sing songs, pray, and learn more about Me. It's a place where people encourage each other to live in a way that shows My love to the world. I'm in every smile, every song, and every prayer. Isn't that wonderful?

And here's the best part—I'm with you when you worship, laugh, and dance! I want you to grow in your understanding of just how much I care for you. Never forget, I'm your Comforter, Helper, and Friend. I'll guide you and fill your heart with joy.

Remember: The Holy Spirit is your comforter and helper.

Bible Treasure: *Meanwhile, the church had peace throughout Judea, Galilee and Samaria, and grew in strength and numbers. The believers learned how to walk in the fear of the Lord and in the comfort of the Holy Spirit."* (Acts 9:31 TLB)

March 27

Hi, My Wonderful Child,

It's Me, your Guiding Spirit, and I want to share a secret: your church leaders need *you*! Yes, you! They work hard to make your church where everyone can worship, learn, and feel My love. Your pastor preaches, visits the sick, and helps people in happy and sad times. Your teachers plan fun and inspiring lessons to help you grow in faith. The musicians practice beautiful songs to lead you in worship, and others work behind the scenes to keep the church clean, safe, and organized.

So, how can you help? You can pray! Prayer is powerful, and I love to hear your prayers. Ask your parents to help you learn the names of your church leaders. Then, pray for each one by name. Pray that I will give them strength, joy, and wisdom. And don't forget to let them know you're praying for them—it will make their hearts so happy!

When you pray, you're helping to build a strong, loving church. You're also showing Me how much you care about the people who serve in My name. Together, we can do amazing things!

Remember: Pray for your church leaders every day.

Bible Treasure: *"Paul and Barnabas also appointed elders in every church and prayed for them with fasting, turning them over to the care of the Lord in whom they trusted."* (Acts 14:23 TLB)

March 28

Hi, My Precious Child,

I have something exciting to tell you—you have a very special name! You are called a *Christian* because you follow Jesus Christ, the chosen one of God. I was with Jesus when He was baptized in the Jordan River, showing He is part of Me. And guess what? When you believe in Him, you become part of My family too!

Your name as a Christian tells the world something beautiful: you believe in Jesus and want to live like Him. One way to do that is by welcoming people who visit your church. When someone new walks through the doors, treat them like a new friend, brother, or sister. Imagine how it feels to walk into a strange place and be greeted with smiles and kindness—that's what I want you to do!

When you welcome others in My name, you're not just being kind but bringing glory to Me. You're showing the world what My love looks like. That's powerful, and it makes Me so proud of you!

Remember: You are a Christian because you follow Jesus Christ.

Bible Treasure*: "So warmly welcome each other into the church, just as Christ has warmly welcomed you; then God will be glorified."* (Romans 15:7 TLB)

March 29

Hi, My Amazing Child,

It's Me, the Holy Spirit, and I have something extraordinary to share about the word *church*! Did you know it can mean two things? Sometimes, it's the building where people gather to worship Me. Churches can be tall, grand, tiny, peaceful, or look like warehouses. Some people worship Me outside, surrounded by trees and skies, while others watch church at home on their TVs or devices. Isn't it amazing how many ways people gather to honor Me?

But here's something even more astonishing: *church* also means *the people*. Wherever people gather to love Me, pray, sing, and learn about Me, they are the church. People of all shapes, colors, and languages from all over the world make up My church. That means you are part of something much bigger than you can imagine—you are My church, and I am with you wherever you go.

So, whether you're in a big building, a small one, or worshiping at home, remember that you and everyone who loves Me are My church. Together, you make Me so proud!

Remember: The church is both a place and the people.

Bible Treasure: *"Let us not neglect our church meetings, as some people do, but encourage and warn each other, especially now that the day of his coming back again is drawing near."* (Hebrews 10:25 TLB)

March 30

Hi, My Beautiful Child,

I care about *you*, not your clothes. Do you think what you wear to church matters to me? It doesn't! What matters is that you come to worship Me with an open heart and a joyful spirit.

Some people like to dress up for church, and that's wonderful. Others might wear the same clothes they wear to school or outside to play, and that's perfectly fine, too. Not everyone has fancy clothes, and that's okay. What's most important is that you're there, ready to learn, sing, and celebrate My love for you. I look at what's on the inside— your thoughts, your kindness, and your passion—not what you wear outside.

And here's something you can do for Me: be kind to everyone, no matter how they dress. Never make fun of someone with worn-out clothes—they might be doing the best they can. Instead, show them My love with your smiles and kindness. That's what makes Me happiest.

Remember: What is in your heart is more important than what is on your back.

Bible Treasure: *"If a man comes into your church dressed in expensive clothes and with valuable gold rings on his fingers, and at the same moment another man comes in who is poor and dressed in threadbare clothes..."* (James 2:2 TLB)

March 31

Hi, My Sacred Heart,

I want you to know something amazing: you can hear My voice everywhere in your church! I speak through your pastor's prayers and sermons. You can listen to Me in the songs sung by the choir and the congregation as they fill the air with praise. When your Church School teachers tell you stories from the Bible, those are My words teaching you about how I've been working in the world for a long time. I'm even in baptism, wrapping My love around babies and adults as they receive My promises.

When you go to church, look around and listen closely. Every prayer, song, and smile is all Me showing My love to you and everyone else. I'm alive in every church, filling people's hearts worldwide. And here's the best part: I'm alive in *your* heart, too.

When you leave church, you're never leaving Me behind. I go with you, wherever you are, always.

Remember: God is with you even when you're not in church.

Bible Treasure: *"Let all who can hear listen to what the Spirit says to the churches."* (Revelation 2:29 TLB)

DON'T BE
AFRAID.
MY CHILD.
I WILL PROTECT YOU
AND BLESS YOU.
GENESIS 15:1 TLB

April 1

Hi there, My fearless child!

Are you feeling scared? It's okay. Everyone feels afraid sometimes—I gave you those feelings to keep you safe! Think about it: if you weren't scared of falling, you might climb too high and get hurt. And loud noises? They can be a warning to pay attention because something important is happening.

But guess what? I am *always* with you, even when you're scared. I'm like a strong, gentle shield, keeping you safe. When you feel afraid, talk to Me. Whisper a prayer, and I will give you peace and courage.

If something makes your heart feel small and shaky, tell someone you trust, like your mom, dad, or a teacher. They can help you understand what's scaring you. Did you know that many fears come from not knowing the truth? Once you know what's real, you'll see—most things aren't as scary as they seem.

So, when you're afraid, remember: *you are never alone.* I am holding your hand, ready to help you face anything.

Remember: Fear may come, but God's love is *always* bigger.

Bible Treasure: "Don't be afraid, My child. I will protect you and bless you."(Genesis 15:1 TLB)

April 2

Hi there, My fantastic child!

Do you ever wonder what you'll be when you grow up? Maybe you have a big dream—like being a scientist, a teacher, an artist, or even an astronaut. But sometimes, little whispers of doubt creep in: *What if I'm not good enough? What if I can't do it?*

Let Me tell you something important: I made you *wonderfully* and gave you talents and dreams for a reason! Doubts might try to make you afraid of the future, but you don't have to listen to them. When you feel unsure, come talk to Me. I *love* hearing your hopes, dreams, and even your fears.

When you pray, I'll give you the courage and confidence to do your best. You don't need to figure everything out— take one step at a time. Dream big, work hard, and trust that I will help you with the rest.

So, be bold, My child! I am with you, and I will never let you go.

Remember: When you talk to Me, your doubts get smaller, and your dreams get bigger.

Bible Treasure: "Be strong and brave! Don't let fear or doubt stop you. I am always with you wherever you go." (Joshua 1:9 TLB)

April 3

Hi there, My brave child!

Do the shadows in your room sometimes seem spooky when the lights go out? Maybe you think you see something hiding in the corner or hear a funny noise, and your imagination starts running wild. But guess what? There are no monsters under your bed or Boogie Men in your closet. It's just your mind playing tricks on you.

Here's a secret: when you're afraid, *turn on the light.* Darkness can't stick around when light shows up! And do you know what? *I am your Light.* Like a lamp chases shadows, I can chase away your fears.

Whenever you feel scared, call out to Me. Talk to Me in prayer, and I'll wrap you in My love and peace. It's like holding My hand through the night—you might not see Me, but I am *always* there. My light is brighter than any fear, and I will keep you safe.

You'll outgrow these fears one day, but until then, lean on Me. I'll never leave you, not even for a second.

Remember: You're never alone. God's light shines even in the darkest night.

Bible Treasure: *"The Lord is my light and my salvation—whom shall I fear?"* (Psalm 27:1 TLB)

April 4

Hello, My amazing child!

Do the shadows on your wall still make you feel scared? Maybe they look like spooky monsters, aliens, or ghosts when the lights are out. But here's a secret: shadows are *pretend*. They're reflections of real things—like trees, toys, or even your clothes on a chair. They can't hurt you and are not as powerful as they seem.

Fear works the same way. It can make things feel much bigger and scarier than they are. But you don't have to face those fears alone—I'm right here with you! When you're afraid, please close your eyes and imagine Me standing beside you. I'll hold your hand, protect you, and fill your heart with courage.

If the shadows still worry you, ask someone you trust—like your mom or dad—to check them out. You'll see there's nothing to be afraid of after all.

So, the next time fear tries to sneak in, remember: I am your strength and will help you chase those fears away. I'm bigger than *any* shadow.

Remember: Shadows can't hurt you. God's light is always with you.

Bible Treasure: *"I prayed to the Lord, and He answered me. He freed me from all my fears."*(Psalm 34:4 TLB)

April 5

Hi there, My bright child!

Have you ever done something wrong and felt like hiding? Maybe you broke something, told a lie, or made a mistake. You might want to keep it a secret, but hiding only makes the fear grow bigger. Guess what? You don't have to hide from Me or your parents. I already know what happened, and I love you *no matter what.*

Everyone makes mistakes—it's part of being human! That's why I created forgiveness. When you mess up, come to Me. Tell Me what happened, and I'll help you make it right. You can also talk to someone you trust, like your mom, dad, or a teacher. You'll feel much better when you stop hiding and face the truth.

Fear likes to whisper, "What if you get in trouble?" But I promise: telling the truth is *always* the best choice. There might be consequences, but there will also be forgiveness, love, and peace. My light will shine brightly in your heart when you're honest.

So don't hide, My child. Step into My light, and let's fix it together.

Remember: Mistakes happen, but God's love and forgiveness are always bigger.

Bible treasure: "*They stayed away from the Light for fear their sins would be exposed.*" (John 3:20 TLB)

April 6

Hi there, My fantastic child!

Did you know you're part of *My* family? That's right! You are My spiritual child, as is everyone else in the world. We're one big family, connected by My love. Isn't that cool?

When you mess up or do something wrong, you might think, *"Uh-oh, I'm in big trouble!"* But don't let that fear keep you from asking for help. I'm here for you—always! Come talk to Me in prayer when you're worried or don't know what to do. I'll fill your heart with peace and guide you to the correct answer.

Sometimes, I'll nudge you to tell an adult you trust—like your mom, dad, or a pastor. Why? Because they've been through tough things, too, and they can help you figure things out. You don't have to face your problems alone!

So don't be afraid, My child. You belong to Me, and I will always help you. My family—your family—is full of love, understanding, and wisdom.

Remember: You're never alone. You're part of God's family, and help is always coming!

Bible Treasure: *"We are God's very own children, adopted into His family, and we call Him, 'Father!'"* (Romans 8:15 TLB)

April 7

Hello, My Sacred Heart!

Did you know that you are *Mine* forever? That's right—you belong to Me, and nothing can ever change that! How? Because of Jesus. Jesus came to earth, lived a perfect life, died on the cross, and came back to life so that you could be part of My family forever.

When you were baptized or when you said, "Jesus, I believe in You," something amazing happened: you were born again in your spirit. You became part of Jesus' life—*His story is now yours!*

You don't have to be afraid of anything. I will be with you daily as you grow up, learn, laugh, and live. And someday, when it's time, you'll be with Me and Jesus in heaven forever. You are never alone—not for one second!

So stand tall, My child. Let your faith in Me make you strong and brave. Live your life with joy, knowing that I'll never leave you. You're Mine, and I will love you always!

Remember: You are part of God's family forever. Nothing can take His love away!

Bible Treasure: *"You belong to Christ, so be free from fear."* (1 Corinthians 7:23 TLB)

April 8
Palm Sunday

Hey there, My fun-loving child!

Today is such an exciting day—Palm Sunday! Do you know what that means? It's a day to celebrate Jesus like the people of Jerusalem did when He came into their town. So, let's get moving! Jump up, stomp your feet, clap your hands, and shout, "Hosanna!" If you've got palm branches, wave them high. If not, wave your hands like you're swatting flies. Let's make some joyful noise together!

Imagine this: Jesus riding into Jerusalem on a donkey. The people were so thrilled to see Him that they lined the streets like it was the best parade ever! They threw down their coats and laid branches on the road, all for Him. They were so excited—they couldn't help but cheer! And guess what? I filled their hearts with joy, just like I'm here with you now.

I love it when you get excited about Jesus, too. Every time you think of Him or whisper a prayer, you invite Him into your heart, which brings Me so much joy.

Remember: Jesus is always with you, ready to bring love, peace, and happiness into your life. Let's keep celebrating Him—today and every day!

Bible Treasure: The two disciples did as Jesus said, [7] and brought the animals to him and threw their garments over the colt for him to ride on. [8] And some in the crowd threw down their coats along the road ahead of him, and others cut branches from the trees and spread them out before him. (Matthew 21:6-8 LBT)

April 9
Monday

Hello, My precious child!

Do you know how special it is when you come to My house? That's what church is—My house! I love being with you wherever you go, but there's something wonderful about people gathering together to worship Me. It's where My children sing songs, pray, and hear stories about My love. Isn't that amazing?

Big things happen in My house! Babies are baptized, couples promise to love each other forever, and lives are celebrated when someone comes home to Me. Church is where you can feel My presence in every prayer, every song, and every smile.

So, when you're in My house, show kindness, listen well, and be respectful. Your good behavior is a beautiful way of saying, "I love You, Lord." It makes My heart so happy to see you honoring what happens in My house.

Remember: The church is a place of joy, love, and prayer—where we can be close together. Come as often as you can!

Bible Treasure: Jesus went into the Temple, drove out the merchants, and knocked over the money changers' tables and the stalls of those selling doves. [13] "The Scriptures say my Temple is a place of prayer," he declared, "but you have turned it into a den of thieves." (Matthew 21:12-13 TLB)

April 10

Tuesday

Hello, My good friend!

Have you ever felt betrayed? That's a big word, but it means someone did something hurtful behind you. On this Tuesday of Holy Week, Judas betrayed Jesus. He went to people who hated Jesus and gave them secret information— just for money. It was a terrible thing to do. I hope you never face something like that, My dear one.

Friendship is one of My greatest gifts to you. It's essential to stay close to and care for your friends. Think about all the fun times you've had together—laughing, playing, helping each other. Those memories remind you how special they are. When you focus on the good things, you'll want to protect your friendship and never do anything to hurt them.

Remember, My child, friends are like treasures. They bring joy, comfort, and love to your life. Treat them with kindness and stay close to them—they are a gift from Me that will make your life brighter.

Remember: I'm always here to help you love others, just as Jesus loves you. Together, let's make your friendships strong and full of joy!

Bible Treasure: Then Judas Iscariot, one of the twelve apostles, went to the chief priests [15] and asked, "How much will you pay me to get Jesus into your hands?" And they gave him thirty silver coins. (Matthew 26:14-15 TLB)

April 11
Wednesday

Hello, My quiet child.

I know you love to move, play, and explore, but today, I have a unique challenge for you. Can you sit still and quietly like a gentle breeze on a calm day? No, you're not in trouble! You didn't do anything wrong. I want to show you something amazing.

Sitting quietly and closing your eyes, you step into a world of stillness. No touching, no looking, no listening to the sounds around you—just you and Me. In this quiet moment, you can feel My love filling your heart.

Let's try this together: close your eyes and say, "Jesus loves me." Repeat it. Now, repeat it nine more times. Let those words sink deep into your heart like a hug from Me.

How do you feel? Peaceful? Loved? That's Me reminding you that no matter what happens, I'm always here, loving you endlessly.

Remember: Even when nothing or no one is around you, Jesus still loves you.

(The Bible does not record any events in the life of Jesus on Wednesday of Holy Week)

April 12
Holy Thursday

Welcome to a Holy Supper, child!

Let me tell you about a fantastic night—Thursday of Holy Week. It was the night Jesus shared a special meal with His disciples called the Last Supper. It wasn't just any meal—the Passover, a celebration of how I helped the Hebrew people escape slavery in Egypt long ago. Thursday night became one of the most critical moments in the lives of Christians everywhere.

At the table, Jesus did something incredible. He took bread, blessed it, broke it, and shared it with His friends. Then He passed around a cup and told them to drink. He said, "Do this to remember Me." That's why today, we have communion or the Lord's Supper. Every time you eat the bread and drink from the cup, it's like sitting at the table with Jesus, just like His disciples did.

When you take communion, My child, feel the love and joy Jesus shared that night. Imagine Him smiling at you, reminding you of His love and sacrifice. It's a beautiful way to stay close to Him and remember everything He's done for you.

Remember: Jesus stated Communion on Thursday of Holy Week.

Bible Treasure: Then he took a loaf of bread; and when he had thanked God for it, he broke it apart and gave it to them, saying, "This is my body, given for you. Eat it in remembrance of me." [20] After supper he gave them another glass of wine, saying, "This wine is the token of God's new agreement to save you—an agreement sealed with the blood I shall pour out to purchase back your souls. (Luke 22"19-20 TLB)

April 13
Good Friday

Please don't be sad, My child.

Today might feel like a sad day—it's Friday of Holy Week, the day Jesus died on the cross. But do you know something amazing? This sad Friday is called **Good Friday** because of what Jesus did for you and everyone.

Let Me explain. Sometimes, people do bad things or sin, which separates people from Me. Sin is like a wall that keeps us apart. But Jesus, who loves you so much, came to break down that wall. He sacrificed Himself—He gave His life—so that all your sins could be forgiven. When He died, He took all the bad things with Him. And when He rose on Easter Sunday, He gave you a brand-new, clean heart and forgiven soul.

That means nothing, absolutely nothing, can separate you from My love! Even when you mess up, I'm still here with you, loving and cheering you on.

It's okay if this feels a little hard to understand. Remember this: Jesus died because We love you more than you can imagine. And because of Him, you can always be close to Me.

Remember: Jesus died for everybody's sins.

Bible Treasure: And Jesus replied, "Today you will be with me in Paradise. This is a solemn promise." [44] By now it was noon, and darkness fell across the whole land[f] for three hours, until three o'clock. [45] The light from the sun was gone—and suddenly the thick veil hanging in the Temple split apart. [46] Then Jesus shouted, "Father, I commit my spirit to you," and with those words he died. (23:43-46 TLB)

April 14
Holy Saturday

Sush, My child.

Do you remember sitting quietly earlier this week? That's what Saturday of Holy Week feels like—still and silent. After Jesus died, His friends placed His body in a tomb, which is like an above-ground grave. They carefully wrapped His body, and someone rolled a big, heavy stone in front of the tomb's entrance to keep it safe.

On that Saturday, the whole world felt quiet, like holding its breath. It seemed like nothing was happening. But do you know what? While everyone was waiting, I was busy preparing something that would change the world forever.

When life feels quiet or seems like nothing is happening, remember this: I'm always working, even when you can't see it. Sometimes, My best work happens when no one is looking! Just like I was preparing for Easter Sunday's joy, I'm always preparing good things for you.

So be patient, My lovely child. Even in the quiet, I'm here, loving you and working to help you in ways you can't imagine. Trust Me—I've got something wonderful planned for you, too!

[42] And so, because of the need for haste before the Sabbath, and because the tomb was close at hand, they laid him there. (John 19:42 LTB)

April 15
Easter Sunday

Easter Blessings, My Sacred Heart!

Did you wake up with excitement in your heart? Today is Easter Sunday—the most joyful day of all! This is the day Jesus rose from the dead to give you and everyone a brand-new life free from sin. Isn't that amazing?

Think back to everything we've talked about this week. Holy Week was full of big moments, some sad and hard to understand. But today, all of that leads to something glorious. When Jesus came out of the tomb, He rolled away more than just the stone—He rolled away sin, too!

Sin is like a wall that kept you far from Me. But when Jesus rose, He broke down that wall forever. Now, nothing can keep Me from being close to you. Just like spring brings new life to flowers and trees, Easter brings new life to your soul. I live in you now, My lovely child, and I'll always be with you.

Remember: Easter starts your new life with Me, full of love, joy, and hope.

Bible Treasure: But when they arrived they looked up and saw that the stone—a *very* heavy one—was already moved away and the entrance was open! ^{5} So they entered the tomb—and there on the right sat a young man clothed in white. The women were startled, ^{6}but the angel said, "Don't be so surprised. Aren't you looking for Jesus, the Nazarene who was crucified? He isn't here! He has come back to life! Look, that's where his body was lying. (Mark 16:4-7 TLB)

April 16

Hi there, My little lamb!

Can I tell you a secret? I love animals! Do you have a favorite animal? Maybe you like playful puppies that give slobbery kisses or snuggly kittens that purr when cozy on your lap. Me? I love little lambs. Do you know why? Because they remind Me of you!

Yes, *you* are one of My precious little lambs. I'm your Shepherd, and I care for you just like a shepherd takes care of a sheep. I watch over you, ensuring you have everything you need to be safe, happy, and loved.

But did you know I have lots of lambs all over the world? Some of them need extra care right now. That's where you can help! When you talk to Me in prayer, tell Me about someone who needs My help. Maybe a friend who's feeling sad or a family member who's sick. Share their name and why they need Me. I promise I'm always listening, and we can care for all My lambs together.

Remember: Because I'm your Shepherd, I will always watch over you!

Bible Treasure: "The Lord is my Shepherd, I have everything I need!" (Psalm 23:1 TLB)

April 17

Hi, My little adventurer!

Do you love playing outside? Isn't it amazing to run through the soft green grass, play games, or fly kites high into the sky? Whether scoring goals, chasing butterflies, or spinning in circles, I love watching you enjoy the warm sunlight and fresh air.

Playing outside isn't just fun—it helps you grow strong and healthy, just as I want you to be. But do you know what else you can do outside? You can talk to Me! Yes, I love it when you take the time to sit quietly with Me. Find a peaceful spot in the grass, or sit by a lake where you can hear the gentle water ripples. That's a perfect time to pray, tell Me about your day, or read your Bible.

Feel the sun on your face? That reminds me, I'm right there with you, smiling as you play or pray. Everything outdoors—the breeze, the trees, the birds—was made for you to enjoy and to help you feel closer to Me.

Remember: You can play and pray outside; God enjoys the outdoors, too.

Bible Treasure: "He lets me rest in the meadow grass and leads me beside the quiet streams." (Psalm 23:2 TLB)

April 18

Hi, My tired child.

Do you ever feel so tired or sick that you don't have the energy to play? I know those days can feel long and hard, but I want you to know something important—I'm here to help you improve.

When your body feels weak, your heart and spirit can feel a little tired, too. That's okay! Everyone needs time to rest and heal. While you're resting, why not talk to Me? Whisper a prayer and tell Me how you're feeling. I love to listen, and I'm always ready to help.

Think of prayer as a warm hug for your soul. It reminds you that I'm caring for you, giving you strength, and helping you heal—inside and out. Rest your body, calm your mind, and let Me fill your spirit with new energy.

Even on those quiet, stay-at-home days, you're never alone. I'm here, working to make you strong again.

Remember: God will help you feel better and get stronger.

Bible Treasure: "He gives me new strength. He helps me do what honors him the most." (Psalm 23:3 TLB)

April 19

Hi, My brave little one.

Have you ever felt scared in the dark? Maybe you saw something in the corner of your room—like a pair of glowing eyes! You froze, afraid to breathe, until... oh, it was just your stuffed animal all along! Does that sound familiar?

When it's dark, your imagination can make things seem much scarier than they are. But here's a trick: turn on the light! Light chases away the shadows and helps you see clearly.

And you know what? When life feels scary, you can come to Me in prayer. Like light brightens a dark room, My presence will calm your fears. Maybe you're worried about something you can't see, like the future. That's okay! You don't have to know what tomorrow holds because I'll be with you every step of the way.

Trust Me, My little lamb. I'll be your light and comfort when life feels dark or uncertain. Together, we'll walk through anything—even the scariest valleys—and you'll never be alone.

Remember: Life can be scary; always trust in God.

Bible Treasure: "Even when walking through the dark valley of death, I will not be afraid." (Psalm 23:4 TLB)

April 20

Hi, My traveling buddy!

Have you ever noticed how much fun it is to go somewhere with a friend? A friend can help you find your way, watch out for traffic, and make the trip less lonely. Plus, having someone to talk to makes the journey so much better!

Can I be your friend on life's journey? I'd love to walk with you and help you along the way. When you pray, it's like having a heart-to-heart with Me. Through prayer, you can ask for My guidance, and I'll always answer—sometimes by sending someone to help you, sometimes by giving you a strong feeling in your heart, or even through words in your Bible or devotional time.

I'm closer than you think—always just a prayer away. No matter where life takes you, you'll never have to travel alone because I'm right here, ready to guide, guard, and walk with you every step of the way.

Remember: God is always close to you; talk to God often.

Bible Treasure: "You are close beside me, guarding, guiding all the way." (Psalm 23:4 TLB)

April 21

Hello, My special guest!

Isn't it fun to share a meal with friends? Imagine everyone laughing and talking while you all enjoy a big pizza. It's hard to stay mad at anyone when you're sharing yummy food! I love it when My children come together around a table. It reminds Me of a big, joyful banquet where everyone is welcome.

Did you know you're always My honored guest? Every time you sit down to eat, I'm right there with you, celebrating *you*! Whether it's a simple meal or a big birthday feast with cake and candles, I love seeing you happy, growing stronger, and enjoying the blessings I've given you.

And guess what? I don't wait to celebrate your birthday—I do it daily! Every day is unique because you're special to Me. So, as you enjoy your meals and spend time with friends and family, remember: I'm celebrating you, too. My blessings are overflowing just for you!

Remember: God celebrates every day like it is your birthday.

Bible Treasure: "You provide delicious food for me… You have welcomed me as your guest; blessings overflow!" (Psalm 23:5 TLB)

April 22

Hi, My Sacred Heart!

Did you know I love giving you good things every single day? I want your life full of joy, strength, and learning. Eating healthy foods will help you grow big and strong. Running, jumping, and playing will keep your body full of energy. And when you spend time reading, you'll discover amazing things about the world I've made!

These are My gifts to you, but here's the secret: you need to use them to keep growing. And guess what else? I'm always right beside you, cheering you on! When you take a moment to talk to Me in prayer, that's one of the best blessings of all—it's a special time just for us.

Please live a happy whole life, knowing I'll always be with you. And one day, when the time is right, I have a beautiful place waiting for you with Me in heaven. Until then, let's make the most of every single day together!

Remember: God is with you now and forever.

Bible Treasure "Your goodness and unfailing kindness shall be with me all of my life, and afterwards I will live with you forever in your home." (Psalm 23:6 TLB)

April 23

Hello, My playful child!

Did you know I love to watch you play and laugh? It fills My heart with joy to see you having fun. Play is one of My greatest gifts—it's how you explore the world, use your imagination, and make wonderful memories. When you run, climb, or ride your bike, your body gets stronger. Your creativity shines when you pretend to be a firefighter or a nurse! Playing games with friends teaches you how to share, work together, and make others smile. Even when you're playing alone, solving puzzles or dreaming big, I'm right there with you.

I created you to enjoy life, and play is an essential part of it. So laugh out loud, shout for joy, and enjoy every moment! Your parents are there to keep you safe, and I always watch over you with love.

Never forget how to play, My dear one. Some people grow up and forget how wonderful it feels to have fun. But not you. Keep playing, keep laughing, and keep shining bright.

Remember: God delights in your play, play often.

Bible Treasure: *"The children of Machir, Manasseh's son, played at his feet."* (Genesis 50:23 LTB)

April 24

Hello, My magical musician!

Do you love to sing and dance? I do, too! When you sing, it brings so much joy to My heart. Your voice is a gift, and it's beautiful just the way it is. I love hearing you sing your favorite songs, and I hope you'll also sing songs about Me. Those songs remind you of My love and fill your heart with peace and happiness. Keep them close, and they'll comfort you whenever you need it.

Dancing is just as unique! I smile when I see you spinning, jumping, and moving joyfully. Did you know that even My children in the Bible sang and danced to celebrate? Music has always been a way to show love, to share happiness, and to worship Me.

Let your voice shine if you sing at school, church, or home! Learn new songs, especially the ones that tell of My love. Sing with your family, and let your home overflow with music and laughter.

Music is My gift to you—it inspires, uplifts, and connects you to Me. So laugh, sing, and dance every day!

Remember: Singing can inspire you and give praise to God.

Bible Treasure: *"His daughter ran to meet him, playing a tambourine and dancing for joy."* (Judges 11:34 LBT)

April 25

Hello, My little drummer!

Do you love music as much as I do? Music fills the world with joy, and it's even more fun when you create it yourself. You don't need a fancy instrument to play music—you can make music with almost anything! Do you have a box or a ball? What about a spoon or a stick? Ask your mom if you can borrow a spoon, and let's turn your box or ball into a drum!

Now, tap your drum and count out loud, "One and two and three and four." Listen to the beat you're making— it's terrific! See? You're already a musician! If you keep practicing, you'll get even better.

Music is one of My unique gifts to you. It brings joy to your heart and makes My heart happy, too. You can sing, play, or even dance along to your music—it's all worship to Me! King David loved music and even gathered musicians to play and sing for Me with joy and excitement.

So go ahead, make some noise, have fun, and let music fill your life with happiness. Remember, I'm always listening and smiling when you play.

Remember: Music can bring joy to you and God and you.

Bible Treasure" *"They played loudly and joyously on harps, psaltries, and cymbals."* (1 Chronicles 15:16 LTB)

April 26

Hello, My happy child!

Did you know I made all My children love playing? Not just you, but even animals love to play! Baby whales race through the ocean, swimming fast around their mothers. Monkeys swing through the treetops, chasing each other like playing tag with friends. And have you seen squirrels? They dart across the ground, leap into trees, and play tag on the branches. Isn't that amazing?

I gave all My creatures the gift of play because it brings joy and helps you grow strong. When you play, you laugh, run, and share happy moments with others. Playing enables you to make friends, explore the world, and celebrate the beautiful life I've given you.

So run, climb, and laugh out loud! Never forget how wonderful it feels to play. Like the whales in the sea and the squirrels in the trees, you were made to enjoy life and have fun. I love watching you play—it fills My heart with joy!

Remember: God made you to play and have fun.

Bible Treasure: *"And look! See the ships! And over there, the whale you made to play in the sea."* (Psalm 104:26 TLB)

April 27

Hello, My fun-loving child!

Do you have a friend who doesn't like to play the same games as you? That's okay—it just means there's an opportunity to try something new together! Why not ask them what they enjoy? Maybe they love kickball, tag, or a fun board game. Or you could introduce them to your favorite game, like hide-and-seek! Everyone loves a good game of hide-and-seek.

If your friend doesn't like those, try letting them teach you their favorite game. You might discover something exciting and new! Learning a different game can be tricky at first, but you'll have so much fun playing it together with practice. That's the beauty of friendship—it's about sharing joy and finding ways to have fun together.

Playing with others makes games even better. The laughter, teamwork, and memories you share are gifts that I delight in, too! So be kind, patient, and open to trying new things. You're building friendships that will bring joy to both of you.

Remember: Games are more fun when played with friends.

Bible Treasure: *"We played wedding and you weren't happy, so we played funeral but you weren't sad."* (Matthew 11:16-17 TLB)

April 28

Hello, My sporty child!

Do you love playing sports? Sports can be so much fun! Playing takes practice, whether you're swinging a bat in baseball, swimming your fastest in the pool, or kicking a soccer ball. To be great at any game, you must train your body, learn the rules, and keep trying daily. It's not always easy, but the more you practice, the better you get—and the more fun you have!

Did you know being a Christian is a lot like that? Just like you practice sports, you can practice your faith every day. Read stories from the Bible, talk to Me in prayer, sing songs about My love, and worship joyfully. You can even make it fun—play games, read exciting books, or share what you've learned with friends. Practicing your faith helps you grow closer to Me and live a life that honors Me.

I love watching you learn, grow, and have fun. Life with Me is a joyful adventure, and every step you take brings you closer to My heart.

Remember: Christians can have fun and play games, too.

Bible Treasure: *"So I run straight to the goal with purpose in every step. I fight to win."* (1 Corinthians 9:26 TLB)

April 29

Hello, My Sacred Heart!

Did you have fun learning new things this week? I hope so! I want you to know that being a Christian is anything but boring. Living a life that honors Me is an adventure full of joy, friendship, and discovery. You can play games with your friends, learn about others who share your faith, and grow into the amazing person I created you to be.

You are unique—one of a kind. I made you for a special purpose, like a musical instrument playing a beautiful tune. You have a voice and a life that can inspire others. Just be yourself! Live with kindness, honesty, and love, and people will see that you're one of My treasured children.

You don't have to try to be "more special" or impress anyone. You're already incredibly special to Me just the way you are. Remember, your life is like a song that brings joy to the world and glory to Me.

Remember: You are unique in God's sight.

Bible Treasure: *"For no one will recognize the tune the flute is playing unless each note is sounded clearly."* (1 Corinthians 14:7 TLB)

ANGER

EVEN ISAAC DOLLES WITH FIGHTS AND FIGHERS
BUT HE KEEP MOVING FORWARD
— GENESIS'S 26:2

April 30

Hey there!

Do you ever feel your face getting hot, your heart beating fast, and this fiery feeling bubbling up inside? That's anger—it's something I've given all My kids, even you. But listen closely because I want to help you understand it.

Anger isn't destructive on its own—it's like a bit of alarm. When something unfair or wrong happens, anger can give you the courage to speak up or the strength to protect someone. Imagine standing up for a friend who's being teased or fixing something that's broken. That's anger doing its job, and it's a good thing!

But here's the secret: anger is like fire. It's useful for a moment, but holding onto it too long can burn you and the people you care about. Don't let anger build walls between you and others. Instead, let it inspire you to make things right and let it go.

I'm always here to help you handle anger with wisdom and love. Together, we can turn what feels wrong into something beautiful.

Remember: Anger isn't meant to stay—it's meant to spark change.

Bible Treasure: *(Genesis 26:21 – Even Isaac dealt with fights and anger, but he kept moving forward!)*

May 1

Hello, My precious child.

I need you to know something: I get angry sometimes. But My anger is never against you. I feel angry when people are hurt, when someone is mistreated, or when kindness is missing. Imagine a friend at school being bullied—does that make you upset? It makes Me upset, too. I love all My children, and it hurts My heart when one of them feels small or scared because of unkindness.

When you feel angry, what do you do? Do you stomp your feet, cry, or maybe even break something? I gave you the feeling of anger and the power to choose how to use it. Anger isn't destructive—it's like a spark! You can use it to light a fire of courage to stand up for what's right or let it burn out of control and hurt others.

When I get angry, I don't hurt people. Instead, I show them a better way—a way of love, fairness, and kindness. That's how I want you to use your anger, too: to make the world a brighter, better place.

Remember: Anger is a tool that helps you protect what's good but never to harm.

Bible Treasure: "No, Lord! Don't punish me in the heat of your anger." (Psalm 6:1 TLB)

May 2

Hello, My calm child.

Let's talk about anger—it's something everyone feels, even you. But how long do you hold onto it? Anger is like having a heavy bag. The longer you carry it, the more tired and unhappy you become. If you let it go, you'll feel so much lighter.

Sometimes, your family or friends might do something that upsets you. It's okay to feel mad for a little while but don't let anger stay in your heart too long. Holding onto anger can turn into something called a grudge. A grudge is like a shadow that follows you, keeping you from feeling happy.

Here's what I want you to do: go and talk to the person who upset you. Maybe they didn't realize what they did hurt you. Perhaps they're ready to say, "I'm sorry." When you talk, you can fix things and feel better. Wouldn't you rather laugh, play, and sing together than stay angry?

Remember: Let the anger go quickly, and joy will follow.

Bible Treasure: "His anger lasts a moment; his favor lasts for life! Weeping may go on all night, but in the morning there is joy." (Psalm 30:5 TLB)

May 3

Hi there, My shining star!

Let's discuss something important—getting along with the people you love. Your family is a big part of your life. You eat together, play together, and maybe even share a room! Imagine how much happier life can be when you treat each other kindly.

Now think about your friends at school. What if everyone was mad at you? Would school feel fun? Probably not. But here's the exciting part: you have the power to make your world a happier place. When you choose kindness, you create joy all around you. It's like planting flowers—the more love and compassion you give, the more beautiful your world becomes.

So, every day, practice spreading happiness. Smile, share, and say kind words. You'll be amazed at how often happiness bounces right back to you! I'm here to help you shine, My love, wherever you go.

Remember: You can make your world bright and full of joy.

Bible Treasure: "The fool who provokes his family to anger and resentment will finally have nothing worthwhile left." (Proverbs 11:29 TLB)

May 4

Hello, My hurried child!

Have you ever felt rushed and angry at the same time? It's like trying to run with your shoelaces untied—you might trip and make a mess! When you're angry, your mind can get so busy thinking about what made you upset that you stop paying attention to what you're doing. That's when mistakes happen.

Imagine you're coloring a beautiful picture, but because you're mad, you color outside the lines or pick the wrong color. That picture doesn't turn out the way you wanted, does it? Anger can do the same thing in your life—it can take over and mess things up if you let it.

But here's the good news: I'm here to help! When you feel angry, stop for a moment and talk to Me. Ask Me to help you calm down and think clearly. I will fill your heart with peace and show you how to handle your feelings better. You can even pray for the person you're upset with—it's amazing how hard it is to stay mad when you're praying for someone!

Remember: Acting out of anger can make things worse, but prayer and peace will make things better.

Bible Treasure: "A wise man controls his temper. He knows that anger causes mistakes." (Proverbs 14:29 LTB)

May 5

Hello, My forgiven child!

I have the best news for you: Jesus took away your sins! Do you know what sins are? They're the things you do that might hurt yourself, someone else, or even Me. But don't be afraid—I didn't send Jesus to make you feel bad. I sent Him because I love you so much and want to forgive you.

I could never stay angry with you. You are My treasure! When you make a mistake, talk to Me. Tell Me you're sorry, and ask for forgiveness. Do you know what I'll say every single time? "I forgive you, My child." That's My promise to you, no matter what.

Do you believe that I forgive you? That's called faith—trusting that My love for you is greater than any mistake. Faith reminds you that you are clean, loved, and forgiven. So, don't hide when you think you've messed up. Run to Me, and I'll fill your heart with peace and joy.

Remember: God doesn't get angry with you. God always forgives.

Bible Treasure: "For God sent Christ Jesus to take the punishment for our sins and to end all God's anger against us." (Romans 3:25 TLB)

May 6

Hello, My sacred heart!

Did you know that Jesus loves you so much that He gave His life to take away your sins and the sins of everyone on Earth? Because of what Jesus did, I can forgive all My children. Isn't that the best news ever?

But I know that sometimes you feel angry when someone does something mean or says something hurtful. Anger can make your heart feel heavy, like carrying a big storm inside you. What can you do when you feel that way?

Come to Me. Lift your hands toward heaven and say, "Holy Spirit, take this anger from me." I promise I will hear your prayer. I will gently take away that anger and replace it with My love. Love is like a warm hug—it feels much better than anger!

Remember, My love can turn any storm in your heart into a rainbow of peace and joy. So the next time you're upset, talk to Me and let Me fill your heart with My love.

Remember: My love is stronger and sweeter than any anger you feel.

Bible Treasure: "So I want men everywhere to pray with holy hands lifted up to God, free from sin and anger and resentment." (1 Timothy 2:8 TLB)

May 7

Hello, My growing child.

I want to share something important with you—something that might feel a little serious, but don't worry, I'm here with you. Let's talk about life and death.

Did you know that everything living—plants, animals, and even people—has a time when their life on Earth ends? Don't be scared! This is part of the beautiful plan I've made. Every moment you're alive is a gift from Me, your Creator. When I made the first human, Adam, I breathed my life into him. That's how precious life is to Me!

Because life is so special, I want you to treasure each day. Play, laugh, love, and notice the world around you. Every sunrise, every smile, and every challenge is a gift for you to enjoy and grow from.

You don't need to fear what comes next—I have a bigger plan than you can imagine. For now, focus on this: Life is My gift to you, and I love you more than ever.

Remember: Every day is a treasure. Live it fully, and thank Me for today's gift.

Bible Treasure: "Every moment of my life was laid out before a single day had passed." (Psalm 139:16 NLT)

May 8

Hello, My dear child.

I want you to know something significant: you don't need to be afraid of death. You have so much life ahead of you, and I am with you daily.

When you wake up in the morning, I'm ready to guide you through your adventures. When you go to bed at night, I watch over you, keeping you safe and sound as you sleep. I will always hold your hand from your first to your last breath. You are never alone.

Each day is a gift from Me—so let's enjoy it together! Laugh, play, explore, and be filled with wonder. When your time on Earth is done (a very long time from now), I'll still be with you, walking hand in hand into heaven, where joy never ends.

So don't worry about what's far away. Celebrate your beautiful life right now, knowing that My love surrounds you always.

Remember: I'm with you today, tomorrow, and forever.

Bible Treasure: "Even when walking through the dark valley of death, I will not be afraid, for you are close beside me, guarding, guiding all the way." (Psalm 23:4 TLB)

May 9

Hello, My prayerful child.

Have you ever known someone who was very sick—maybe a parent, grandparent, or friend? When someone isn't feeling well, your prayers are powerful! You can talk to Me and ask Me to help them feel better, to heal their body, and to give them strength. I love to hear your prayers because they come straight from your heart.

Sometimes, though, people are very sick and won't recover. This is called being terminally ill. That can sound sad or scary, but remember what I've told you: I am always with them. Whether they are getting better or preparing to come home to heaven, I stay close by their side.

When you pray for someone who is sick, you are helping them feel My love and comfort. Your prayers are like a warm hug from both of us, reminding them they are never alone. And guess what? Your prayers also keep them close to you in a very special way.

Remember: Always pray for the sick. Your prayers make a big difference!

Bible Treasure: "Please come and place your hands on her and make her live." (Mark 5:23 TLB)

May 10

Hello, My forgiven child.

Have you ever wondered why people die? It all began with the very first person, Adam. When Adam disobeyed Me, sin entered the world. Sin is like a wall that separates people from Me, and because of it, Adam couldn't stay in My perfect presence. He began to grow old, and one day, he died. That made Me so sad because I love all My children.

But I had a plan to bring you back to Me! I sent My Son, Jesus, to fix what sin broke. Jesus paid the price for all the wrong things people have done and ever will do. When you are baptized, I come to live in your heart, and you are never far from Me—not for one second.

One day, you will live with Me forever in heaven, where there is no more sadness, pain, or death. You'll be with everyone you love who knows Me, too. Sin may have caused separation, but Jesus made us one family again. You are always Mine!

Remember: Sin separates, but Jesus brings us back together.

Bible Treasure: "When Adam sinned, sin entered the entire human race. His sin spread death throughout all the world." (Romans 5:12 TLB)

May 11

Hello, My eternal child.

I want you to know something very special: I forgive your sins. When you make mistakes or do something wrong, I never stop loving you—not for a moment. My heart is big enough to forgive anything because My love for you is endless.

When you mess up, don't be afraid to come to Me. Tell Me everything in prayer—what you did, how you feel—and I will forgive you completely. That's My promise! You'll feel much lighter and happier when you let go of the wrong and receive My forgiveness.

I don't want anything to come between us. I want to bless you and fill your heart with love, not punish you. Remember, My forgiveness is always waiting for you. Just talk to Me honestly, and we'll walk forward together. You're My child, and nothing can change that.

Remember: I want to forgive and free you from anything that separates us.

Bible Treasure: "All praise to him who always loves us and who set us free from our sins by pouring out his lifeblood for us." (Revelation 1:5 TLB)

May 12

Hello, My precious child.

I know it can feel scary or sad, but I want you to know the truth: you never need to be afraid. I am always with you. All things die. But you will live forever in Me.

When someone you love dies, it doesn't mean they are gone forever. It means they've come to live with Me in heaven, where there's no pain, sadness, or tears—only joy and love. Heaven is a wonderful place, and I've prepared it for everyone who loves Me.

Your job is to live the beautiful life I've given you. Laugh, play, love others, and remember that every moment is a gift from Me. When it's your time—far in the future—I will hold your hand and bring you safely home to heaven.

You are My child, and I promise to be with you every step of your life.

Remember: Death is not the end; it's the beginning of forever with Me.

Bible Treasure: *"He will wipe away all tears from their eyes, and there shall be no more death, nor sorrow, nor crying, nor pain. All of that has gone forever."* Revelation 21:4 TLB.

May 13

Hello, My Sacred Heart.

Let's talk about something very special today—heaven! Did you know that heaven is My home, filled with so much love, joy, and peace that it's beyond what you can imagine? One day, far in the future, you'll join Me there, and it will be amazing.

You might wonder what happens when someone you love dies. Even though it can make you feel sad, I want you to remember that death isn't the end—it's a new beginning. When someone comes to heaven, they are happy, healthy, and surrounded by My love. They are never alone, and neither are you.

For now, I want you to enjoy the life I've given you. Every sunrise, every laugh, and every hug is a reminder of how much I love you. And when it's time—many years from now—I'll take your hand and bring you home to heaven, where we'll be together forever.

Remember: Heaven is a wonderful place, and I will always be with you—here and there.

Bible Treasure: "Jesus told her, 'I am the one who raises the dead and gives them life again. Anyone who believes in me, even though he dies like anyone else, shall live again.'" (John 11:25 TLB)

May 14

Hello, My hurting one.

Have you ever felt a deep ache because someone you love isn't with you anymore? When someone dies, it's okay to feel sad. I feel sad, too, because I love each of My children so much. I watched them grow, laugh, and live their lives— each special to Me.

That sadness you feel. It has a name. It's called grief. Grief is like a heavy cloud in your heart. It makes you feel like something important is missing, like a puzzle with a piece gone. You might feel it deep in your tummy or even all over. It's okay to feel this way, My child. It just shows how much you love.

But grief isn't stronger than love. Love is forever, and I'm here to help you carry your sadness. Talk to someone you trust—a parent, a teacher, or a friend. And talk to Me too. I'm always ready to listen when you pray, to comfort you, and to remind you that you are never alone.

Remember: I promise we will get through this together.

Bible Treasure: "*I am weary from grief; strengthen me through Your word.*" (**Psalm 119:28**)

May 15

My dear searching child,

I know how heavy your heart can feel when someone you love is no longer with you. That feeling of sadness? It's called grief. I gave you grief because your heart needs a soft place to rest when you lose someone you care about deeply. Grief is like love's saying, "I'm not ready to let go."

You loved that person (or even that special animal) so much, and now they're gone. But guess what? Love doesn't disappear. It changes into memories and helps you hold onto all the good times you shared.

When you're grieving, I'm always here to comfort you. I send family and friends to listen, hug you tight, and remind you that you're still surrounded by love. When you pray to Me, I'll tell your heart how much I love you. Over time, I'll even help you smile when you think about the person you lost.

Remember, grief is part of the love I've placed in you. And My love? It's always here to carry you through.

Bible treasure: *"Although He brings grief, He will show compassion because of His great love."* (**Lamentations 3:32**)

May 16

Hello, My musical child.

Do you have a favorite song? Isn't it amazing how music can make you feel happy and peaceful or even help you remember something special? Did the person you loved—now in Heaven—have a favorite song? Maybe even your pet has a song that makes you think of them. Music is like a magical hug for your heart, bringing back wonderful memories.

When you're sad, listen to a song that reminds you of your loved one. Close your eyes and let the music bring those good memories to life. It's okay to smile, laugh, or even cry. Music helps you feel connected to the ones you miss.

Do you like to write? You could write a letter to your loved one. Tell them how much you miss them, love them, or even how their favorite song makes you think of them. You don't have to mail the letter—it's just for your heart. Writing and music are unique ways to hold on to the love you share.

Remember, I'm always here with you, comforting you through every note and word.

Bible treasure: *"Sadly, I sing this song of grief for you."* **(Amos 5:1)**

May 17

Hello, My special child,

When someone you love dies, you're not the only one who feels the sadness. Your whole family and even your friends will grieve, too. But here's something important to remember: everyone grieves in their way. Some people cry a lot, while others might seem quiet or keep their feelings inside. That's okay. Grief looks different for everyone because I made each of My children unique.

You might notice your feelings differ from those of your siblings or parents. That's normal! It's kind and brave to ask if you're unsure how someone is doing. And don't be afraid to share how you're feeling, too. Talking about your sadness can make your heart feel lighter.

Remember, I am always here for you. When you pray, I'm listening closely, ready to bring comfort and remind you of all the happy memories you shared with your loved one. Those memories are treasures, like little gifts from Heaven.

Remember: Grieving takes time, but you don't have to go through it alone. You are deeply loved, My child.

Bible Treasure: "*The whole nation will be bowed down with universal grief... each family will go into private mourning.*" (Zechariah 12:12-14)

May 18

Hi Again, My sweet child.

Did you know that grief doesn't just make your heart feel heavy? It can affect your whole body, too. When someone you love dies, you might feel extra tired or not want to eat. You might not like playing games, watching your favorite shows, or doing anything you usually enjoy. Some of My children sleep often, while others have trouble falling asleep.

Grief can also make your spirit feel a little broken. You might feel angry at Me, thinking I caused your loved one's death. But hear this: I didn't cause it. I love you and care for your loved ones here in Heaven. Please talk to Me in your prayers and tell Me how you're feeling. I want to hear every word.

Talking to a parent or trusted adult is essential if you're not feeling like yourself. Grown-ups grieve, too, so you're not alone. Some so many people love you and want to help.

Remember: Grief is very difficult, but you're never alone. I'm here, holding you close.

Bible Treasure: *"At last, He returned to the disciples and found them asleep, exhausted from grief."* (**Luke 22:45**)

May 19

Hello, My celebrating child.

Did you know that so many people loved the person you loved? Some of their friends or family might have lived far away, so you may not have met them. But when someone you love dies, there's often a special gathering called a funeral. It's a time when everyone comes together to celebrate the life of the person you loved.

You'll hear stories about your loved one at a funeral—things you might not have known! Strangers might tell you funny or heartwarming memories, and you'll realize how special they were to so many people. It's also a time to say goodbye, which can help your heart feel a little lighter.

You might hear about Heaven, the wonderful place where I welcome all My children. I love each of you so much, and I bring my children with me forever. When you pray, you can feel closer to your loved one because they're with Me now.

Remember, a funeral isn't just about sadness—it's also about celebrating love, memories, and the joy they brought to your life.

Bible Treasure: *"Great crowds trailed along behind, and many grief-stricken women."* (**Luke 23:27**)

May 20

Hello, My Sacred Heart.

Did you know grief isn't just about losing someone you love? Sometimes, you can feel it when you're afraid of losing something or someone important to you. But here's a secret: worrying about what *might* happen can steal your joy today. I want you to focus on the good things you have right now.

When you grow close to someone, worrying about losing them is easy because you know everything on Earth has a season. But instead of thinking about what might happen someday, cherish your moments with them today. Laugh with them. Love them. That's what life is all about.

Some people worry so much about losing their money or belongings that they forget to enjoy the blessings I've already given them. But guess what? Life is My gift to you; possessions are just extras to make your journey more comfortable. They can be replaced if lost, but your joy and peace are far more precious.

Trust Me with tomorrow, My child. When you have faith in Me, you can let go of fear and enjoy every beautiful moment today brings.

Remember: Enjoy today more by worrying about tomorrow less.

Bible Treasure: "*Look here, you rich men, now is the time to cry and groan with anguished grief.*" (James 5:1)

May 21

Hello, My heavenly child.

I have something fantastic to tell you. I created the earth a long time ago—a special place for you and all My children. I also made the heavens, a word that means everything above the world: the sky, the sun, the moon, the stars, and the planets. But there's also another heaven—a perfect, beautiful place where I live with those who have come to be with Me forever.

Do you know why I did all of this? Because I love you more than you can imagine. My love is so big and strong that nothing in the world could ever take it away. Not one thing! And here's something even more impressive: Heaven is where My love will wrap you up forever. One day, you'll be with Me there, along with your family and friends, united in My love that never ends.

So when you look at the stars, the sky or feel the sun on your face, remember: I made it all for you because I love you. And Heaven? It's My gift of love, waiting for you.

Remember: Heaven is where My love lasts forever!

Bible Treasure: When God began creating the **heaven**s and the earth (Genesis 1:1 TLB)

May 22

Hello, My searching child.

I have a secret to share with you: I am *everywhere*! I'm in the air you breathe and the water you drink. I'm in the tiniest creatures, so small you'd need a microscope to see them, and I'm with the fantastic beasts that roam the earth and swim in the oceans. I'm there in the darkest, deepest part of the ocean and on the tallest, sunlit mountains.

Because I'm everywhere, you never have to look far to find Me. Wherever you are—no matter how far or near—call My name. Talk to Me through prayer, and I'll be right there, listening and wrapping you in My love. Out of all the places I am in this amazing universe, one of My favorites is beside *you*.

So, never feel alone. I'm always here, ready to listen, comfort, and remind you how much I love you.

Remember: The glory of God is everywhere.

Bible Treasure: *"O Lord our God, the majesty and glory of Your name fills all the earth and overflows the heavens."* *(Psalm 8:1 TLB)*

May 23

Hello, My helper.

I want to share something very close to My heart. I hear every cry from My children—the hungry, the hurting, the lost, and the lonely. When they feel sad or afraid, I think it, too. I never meant for life to be so hard, but I've given each of you a powerful gift to make the world brighter: love.

You can help Me by sharing that love, My child. Pray for those who are struggling. Tell your church, school, or your friends, and you can pray for specific children who need help together. Maybe you can even choose a mission project—sending gifts, money, or messages of hope. When people work together, their kindness can do amazing things.

I know you're young but don't need to wait to start helping others. Your prayers, love, and actions can make a big difference. Will you be My helper? Together, we can fill the world with My love.

Remember: You can be a helper for God at any age!

Bible Treasure: *"Oh, that the Lord might look down from heaven and respond to my cry!" (Lamentations 3:50 TLB)*

May 24

Hello, My baptized child.

Do you know I'm always with you? Just as I came down from heaven like a gentle dove to be with Jesus at His baptism, I come to be with you, too. I am the Holy Spirit and desire to stay close to you every moment of the day. My love for you is so big and strong that I can't stand far from you. Can you feel Me with you now? I hope so because I am right here.

When you were baptized, something amazing happened: My Spirit was unleashed in your life. Baptism shows the world that I am working in you, guiding you, and filling you with Your holy power. You are one of My heavenly children, chosen to bring light to the earth.

Heaven isn't just far away, up in the clouds. Heaven is wherever you live by faith and trust in Me. When you do that, heaven is right here with you.

Remember: You were baptized just like Jesus and have Me within you!

Bible Treasure: *After His baptism, as soon as Jesus came up out of the water, the heavens were opened to Him, and He saw the Spirit of God coming down in the form of a dove."* *(Matthew 3:16 TLB)*

May 25

Hello, My twin.

Do you have a mirror nearby? Go ahead, sit in front of it, and take a good look. What do you see? If you said, "I see myself," you might be missing something amazing. Look harder—I want you to see *Me* in you. Not My face, but My work. I want you to reflect on how I love and serve in heaven by how you live on earth.

Acting like Me is simpler than you think. You have to do one powerful thing: *love*. Love My children—every single one of them—the way I love you. My greatest joy in heaven is loving all My children on earth. When you love others like I do, incredible things happen. Hearts soften, friendships grow, and kindness spreads like sunlight breaking through the clouds.

Yes, my love can change the world, but it begins with you. Reflect my love, and watch how your light brightens the lives of others.

Remember: You look most like God when you act like God.

Bible Treasure: *"But you are to be perfect, even as your Father in heaven is perfect." (Matthew 5:48 TLB)*

May 26

Hello, My gifted child.

Did you know you have two kinds of parents? You have your mom and dad, who gave your life on earth, and you have Me, your heavenly parent, who gave you a brand-new spiritual life. Being born again means you've discovered I live within you, guiding and loving you daily.

Do you look more like your mom or dad? You may resemble your earthly parents, but you also reflect Me, your heavenly parent. You "look" like Me when you share love with everyone around you. My passion is what makes you shine!

I've also given you heavenly gifts—special abilities to help serve others and share My love. You might not know your gifts yet, but don't worry. As you grow, I will show you everything you need to live a good life and help bring more people into My family. When you share My love, you're helping Me create more spiritual brothers and sisters. Thank you for being part of My work.

Remember: God needs your help to create heavenly children on earth.

Bible Treasure: *"Men can only reproduce human life, but the Holy Spirit gives new life from heaven." (John 3:6 TLB)*

May 27

Hello, Sacred Heart.

Oh, how I wish I could show you pictures of heaven! But heaven is far too beautiful for any image to capture. Even the words in the Bible, as wonderful as they are, can only give you a tiny glimpse of its glory. Heaven is beyond anything your mind can imagine—more amazing than your favorite dream, more beautiful than the most colorful sunset.

But let Me tell you what heaven truly is: it's where you will be with Me forever. You won't just feel Me in your heart—you'll see Me face to face, and I'll hold you close in My love. Your friends and family who have come to Me will be there too. In heaven, there's no more separation, only joy, love, and togetherness.

You see, heaven isn't just a place I live—it's a part of who I am. I created it out of My pure, everlasting love for you. My love, like heaven, is more precious than anything on earth. And both are My gifts to you.

Remember: Heaven is found at the very heart of God's love.

Bible Treasure: *"And I, John, saw the Holy City, the new Jerusalem, coming down from God out of heaven. It was a glorious sight, beautiful as a bride at her wedding." (Revelation 21:2 TLB)*

YOU WILL SHOW ME

Faithh of Life

In Your presence is fullness of Joy.

— PSALM 16:11 —

May 28

Hello, My Forever Child,

Do you know how much I love you? I made your life a beautiful gift filled with moments of laughter, love, and wonder. One day, when your time on this earth is complete, I'll have another fantastic gift for you—eternal life! That means living with Me forever and ever.

Imagine this: a life where there's no more sadness, hurt, and pain—only joy that bubbles up like a never-ending fountain. The happiest moments you've ever had here are just a tiny taste of what's waiting for you in heaven. I made heaven just for you, and it's even better than you can dream.

But while you're here, I want you to enjoy every day. Look around—see the colors, hear the sounds, and feel the love I've poured into your life. If things ever feel tuff, don't give up. I'm right here with you, cheering you on and helping you every step of the way.

Remember: Eternal life is a loving gift from God.

Bible Treasure: "You will show me the path of life; in your presence is fullness of joy." (Psalm 16:11)

May 29

Hello, My Dreamer,

What do you dream about becoming when you grow up? Maybe a doctor helping people feel better or a teacher who lights up children's minds. Perhaps you want to care for animals as a veterinarian or create art that makes the world more beautiful. Whatever it is, I'm so excited about the fantastic plans I've placed in your heart!

As you grow and chase those dreams, I want you to remember something important: don't forget about Me. I gave you those dreams, and I'll help you reach them. But sometimes, people get so busy with work and making money that they forget what truly matters—Me and the love I've given them. Work and success are excellent, but without Me, something will always feel like it's missing.

I'll be with you every step of the way. When things feel challenging or confusing, lean on Me. I'll help you discover the best path for your life and remind you of what's most important—My love for you and the joy of sharing your life with Me.

Remember: God will help you achieve your goals, so dream big.

Bible Treasure: "What good will it be for someone to gain the whole world, yet forfeit their soul?" (Matthew 16:26)

May 30

Hello, My Eternal Child,

Have you ever thought about forever? It's a big idea. But here's the amazing truth: your forever with Me has already started! Eternal life isn't something that begins far away in heaven; it begins the very day you were born. You are living the first steps of a never-ending adventure with Me.

One day, your life on earth will end but don't be afraid. That's when your heavenly life with Me will continue—a life filled with joy, love, and wonder beyond anything you can imagine.

But here's the best part: eternal life isn't about counting days or years. It's about living every moment with Me, knowing My love for you will never end. When you follow Jesus, trust in My guidance, and let My love shine through you, you're already living in the promise of eternity!

So keep your heart close to Me, My child. I'll help you walk through this life with peace and joy, and when the time comes, I'll guide you into My eternal glory.

Remember: Eternal life starts right now.

Bible Treasure: "Someone came to Jesus and asked, 'Teacher, what good thing must I do to get eternal life?'" (Matthew 19:16)

May 31

Hello, Follower of Jesus,

Do you know how much I love you? I sent Jesus to show you just how deep My love goes. Jesus wasn't just a teacher or a storyteller—He was perfect love in action! When you read about Jesus in your Bible, you'll see how He loved others, helped those in need, and trusted Me completely. That's how much I care about you—I gave you Jesus as the perfect example of love.

But here's something even more impressive: the same Holy Spirit that was with Jesus is with you right now. That's Me! When you pray, read about Jesus, or feel peace in your heart, it's Me reminding you that you're never alone.

Your faith is like a flashlight—it helps you see that My promises are real, even when the path ahead feels dark. Trust in that faith, and you'll understand the incredible gift I've given you: eternal life. Jesus came to show you the way to Me, and I'll guide you every step of the journey.

Remember: Jesus showed us the way to eternal life.

Bible Treasure: "And this is the way to have eternal life— by knowing you, the only true God, and Jesus Christ, the one you sent to earth!" (John 17:3)

June 1

Hello, Did You Receive the Gift I Sent You?

Have you ever wondered why I sent Jesus to the world? It's because I love you so much! I wanted to make a way for you to be with Me forever, and Jesus was the answer. He brought a special message of love, hope, and eternal life.

When you read stories about Jesus in your Bible, you'll see how much He cared for everyone He met. He healed, helped, and showed people how to live in love. But Jesus didn't just teach about My love; He proved it! He gave His life so you and all My children could live with Me forever. And when He rose from the dead, He made the way to eternal life for everyone who believes in Him.

Through Jesus, I've given you the greatest gift—My eternal love and the promise of life that never ends. Believe in Jesus, My child, and know that My love for you is forever.

Remember: Jesus brought the blessings of God's eternal love.

Bible Treasure: "For God loved the world so much that he gave his only Son, so that anyone who believes in him shall not perish but have eternal life." (John 3:16)

June 2

Hello, My Treasure,

Did you know that everything you see on earth—mountains, trees, even buildings—won't last forever? Over time, wind and rain wear them down, and they fade away. Even the tallest mountains will one day become small hills. But there's something that will never fade, break, or end: I've prepared the gift of eternal life for you.

You see, My love is different from anything in this world. It never erodes, decays, or disappears. My love and the life I've promised you lasts forever. Everything is safe and perfect in heaven, held in My holy presence. Nothing can harm the gift I've kept for you in My heart.

So enjoy the beautiful world I've given you now—play, laugh, and explore! But remember, this life is just the beginning of something even greater. I am the keeper of your eternal life, and My love for you will never fail. You are My treasure, and I will hold you close forever.

Remember: God is the keeper of your gift of eternal life.

Bible Treasure: "And God has reserved for His children the priceless gift of eternal life; it is kept in heaven for you, pure and undefiled, beyond the reach of change and decay." (1 Peter 1:4)

June 3

Hello, My Sacred Heart,

I love you so much and want to keep you safe and close to Me every day. Just like I keep My promise of eternal life safe in heaven, I want to keep your heart full of My love as you grow on earth. You'll always feel My presence guiding and comforting you when you stay close to Me.

How can you stay close to Me? Let Me share a few ideas. Spend time with Me by praying—I love hearing your voice and your heart's thoughts. Read your Bible to learn how I've helped others and the wonderful things Jesus taught. And don't forget to worship! Joining others to sing, learn, and share My Love will bring us closer, too.

Most of all, listen to your heart. I'm there, whispering My love for you. You'll feel our closeness when you pray, worship, and read about Me.

Stay with Me, My child, and I will stay with you, guiding you toward the eternal blessings I have waiting for you.

Remember: Stay close to God and receive your heavenly blessings.

Bible Treasure: "Stay always within the boundaries where God's love can reach and bless you. Wait patiently for the eternal life that Jesus Christ in his mercy is going to give you." (Jude 1:21)

June 4

Hello, My growing child!

I want to talk with you about staying strong inside and outside. Think of it like caring for a special garden: your spirit, body, and mind are all part of this beautiful garden I've given you to grow.

Your spirit blooms when you talk to Me in prayer, read My Word and sing songs of praise. Each prayer and worship song is like sunshine for your heart, making it stronger and brighter.

But don't forget your body—it's a gift too! Run, play, jump, and explore outside. I made the world for you to enjoy! Eating colorful, healthy foods like fruits and veggies keeps your body fueled and ready for anything.

And your mind? It's like a treasure chest waiting to be filled! Read books, ask big questions, and practice memorizing verses from the Bible. Learning new things, especially about Me, will make your mind sharper and your heart glad.

When you take care of yourself today, you're preparing for the amazing things I have planned for you tomorrow. Let's grow strong together, My child!

Remember: What you do today may affect how you live tomorrow.

Bible Treasure: "Then his body will become as healthy as a child's, firm and youthful again." (Job 33:25 TLB)

June 5

Are you feeling sick, My Precious child?

I want to remind you of something important: I'm right here with you, even when you're feeling sick, helping you get better.

Sometimes, your body has to face colds, fevers, or the flu as it grows stronger. It's like your body is learning to build its own defense team! When you feel crummy and need to rest, I'm beside you, cheering your body on as it fights back.

While healing, take it easy—snuggle up in bed, read a good book, or talk to Me in your heart. Remember to avoid others so they don't catch what you have. I promise that soon, you'll be up and running again, ready to laugh, play, and learn with your friends.

I love seeing you full of energy, but for now, let Me hold you close and help you feel better. Trust Me—I've got this.

Remember: God will help you get better when you get sick.

Bible Treasure: "O Lord my God, I pleaded with you, and you gave me my health again." (Psalm 30:2 TLB)

June 6

Hello, My fast child!

Have you noticed that some days you may feel better than others? Some days, you'll feel like you can run faster than the wind; other days, you might feel tired or sad. That's okay! Your body and emotions change from time to time. Eating healthy foods, getting good sleep, and moving your body will help you feel your best. Exercise strengthens your muscles so you can do incredible things!

When sadness sneaks in—and it does for everyone—know that you don't have to face it alone. Tell a parent or another trusted adult how you feel. And don't forget to spend time with Me! Praying, reading your Bible, and singing songs of praise can help your heart feel lighter and stronger.

Your mind, body, and spirit are connected, so take care of each part as best as possible. And remember, I'm always by your side, ready to help. Talk to Me anytime—I love hearing from you.

Remember: God is always available to give you strength and support you.

Bible Treasure: "My health fails; my spirits droop, yet God remains! He is the strength of my heart; he is mine forever!" (Psalm 73:26 TLB)

June 7

Hi, My talkative child!

I want to talk with you about something super important: your words. Did you know your words have incredible power? They can make someone smile or even brighten their whole day!

Think about the things you say. Do you tell your mom how much you love her or remind your dad how awesome he is? A kind word is like a little gift—it brings joy to others and spreads happiness around you. Even a simple "thank you" or "great job" can make someone feel special.

But what happens when you grumble or complain? If you whine about dinner, it might seem worse than it is. If you fuss over homework, it might feel more complicated than it is. Complaining creates a gloomy atmosphere, but kind, happy words light up the world around you.

So, let's fill your day with good words! Speak with kindness, think happy thoughts, and watch your world become brighter. Remember, I'm here to help you every step of the way.

Remember: Your thoughts and words influence your mind and mood. Think happy.

Bible Treasure: "Gentle words cause life and health; griping brings discouragement." (Proverbs 15:4 TLB)

June 8

Good morning, My lovely child. You look fantastic this morning. I hope the sun shines for you all day; if it isn't sunny, you can still feel like the golden rays of the sun coming directly to you. How can you feel good when it is bleak and dreary out? You can feel good by telling yourself good things. It will be a good day; chances are you will have a great day. If you remain a gloomy person, your day may feel that way as well.

If you talk to other people with positive words, they will feel your happy energy and have a good day as well. A lot of your health depends on your mood and attitude. How you feel and what you think are linked together at times. What you say to other people and what they think about you are also tied together. Try to say nice things to people, and good things will happen to you and them.

Wake up every morning as say, "God loves me." Those words can be the start of a great day.

Remember

Happy thoughts and words often create a great day.

Kind words are like honey—enjoyable and **health**ful. (Proverbs 16:24 TLB)

June 9

Hello, Active Child!

I want to help you stay healthy—mind, body, and spirit. Let's talk about how we can work together to keep you strong!

Your body is a wonderful gift, so take care of it! Run, jump, and play to keep your muscles strong. Eat healthy foods that fuel your energy and help you grow. And don't forget to get plenty of rest—your body needs sleep to recharge.

Your mind is amazing, too! Fill it with good things by reading books, learning at school, and choosing TV shows that teach you something helpful. Your spirit is just as important, and you can make it strong by talking to Me daily, reading your Bible, and spending time with others who love Me at church.

When you're sick, it's okay to rest and let your body heal. Listen to your parents and the doctor—they're on your team, just like Me. Together, we'll help you grow into the healthy, happy, and strong person I know you can be.

Remember: Do the things that will keep you healthy.

Bible Treasure: "It is the sick who need a doctor, not those in good health." (Luke 5:31 TLB)

June 10

Hello, My p Sacred Heart,

Do you know someone who could use a little extra care? Maybe a friend, a family member, or even a teacher? One of the best ways you can help them is through prayer. Praying for others is like sending them a special gift of love and hope!

Here's an idea: make a prayer list. Write down the names of people you care about, and during your prayer time, say each name out loud. Ask them if there's something specific they'd like you to pray for—maybe they're feeling worried, sad, or need help with something. Letting them know you're praying for them can brighten their day and remind them they're not alone.

You can also help your friends and family stay healthy in other ways! Invite them to play outside, ride bikes, or run around with you. Learn and study together and worship as a group at church. You create a circle of love and strength when you pray, play, and grow together.

Your prayers can inspire others to pray, too. Imagine how many lives you can touch by showing kindness and lifting up people in prayer!

Remember: Pray for others so that God will help them and keep them healthy.

Bible Treasure: "Dear friend, I am praying that all is well with you and that your body is as healthy as I know your soul is." (3 John 1:2 TLB)

June 11

Hello, My hopeful one,

Don't ever let go of hope, My precious one. Hope is like light shining inside your heart, and I keep it glowing! If you lose that light, you've stopped trusting Me to care for you. But guess what? I'm holding your future in My hands and have excellent plans just for you.

Sometimes, life feels like it's not going how you want it to. Maybe you've been waiting for something special to happen, and it hasn't. Don't worry—wait for Me. I'm working behind the scenes to bring good things into your life. It might not happen when you expect it, but I never stop working for your good.

When you give up hope, it's like closing your eyes to all the wonderful surprises I'm preparing for you. Keep watching, keep trusting, and don't miss out! Being patient is part of having hope. When you wait and trust Me, the blessings I send will be just what you need—even if they're not exactly what you thought they'd be.

Remember: Don't give up hope. God isn't done working yet

Bible Treasure: "Can't I rely on your help? Can't you see I'm helpless without you?" (Job 6:13 TLB)

June 12

Are you ready to dream big, My child?

When you feel like giving up on your dreams, that's the perfect time to talk to Me in prayer. Prayer is like your private Wi-Fi connection straight to My heart—it's always there and never goes out! When you pray, you tell Me what's on your mind, and you can also listen for the answers I'm sending back to you. Trust Me, I always answer, but sometimes My answers differ from what you expect.

Come to Me with big dreams and great hope because your imagination is a gift I gave you! Those fantastic ideas about what your future could be? I love hearing them. When you dream and hope, I can help guide you to make those dreams come true. If something doesn't work out, don't worry! I'll help you figure out an even better plan.

The best part about dreaming is that you don't have to do it alone. Share your dreams daily, and we'll work on them together. I can't wait to hear what amazing things you're imagining!

Remember: Your imagination creates the dreams for which you hope.

Bible Treasure: "When I had lost all hope, I turned my thoughts once more to the Lord, and my earnest prayer went to you in your holy Temple." (Jonah 2:7 TLB)

June 13

Hey, wait for Me!

Patience isn't always easy. But it's something I'm helping you grow, little by little. Life doesn't run on your clock—it's much bigger than that. And guess what? I'm never too busy for you. I see and hear you, and I will never forget you. So, take a deep breath and wait with patience. Patience is like planting seeds of faith in your heart.

If you got everything you wanted, exactly when you wanted it, you wouldn't need to trust Me, would you? Faith learns to wait, knowing that I'm always working behind the scenes for your good. Even when nothing is happening, trust Me—I'm making something extraordinary just for you.

As you practice patience, you're building something amazing inside yourself: a stronger faith and a heart that trusts Me completely. The less you worry about what you hope for, the more room you have to believe in My perfect timing. And don't forget—I'll always give you what you need, even if it looks slightly different from what you imagined.

Remember: Faith and trust work together to build spiritual strength.

Bible Treasure: "Patience develops strength of character in us and helps us trust God more... until finally our hope and faith are strong and steady." (Romans 5:4 TLB)

June 14

Hello, My loving child,

Faith is like a doorway, My child—it's how you connect with Me. It helps you think about Me, talk to Me in prayer, and believe I'm always here for you. Without faith, you wouldn't know I exist! But because you believe in Me, you have hope that I'll fill your life with good things in the future. Faith and hope work together like best friends.

But do you know what's even more significant than faith and hope? Love. Love is the greatest thing of all! My love is what connects you to Me and everyone around you. I made you out of love, and I keep blessing you every day because I love you more than you can imagine.

I want you to love others the way I love them. It's not always easy, especially when people make mistakes, but when you forgive them and love them anyway, you share my love. Love isn't just a feeling; it's a gift. When you give someone your love, you're giving them a piece of your heart—and that's the best gift of all.

Remember: Your love is the greatest gift you can give someone.

Bible Treasure: "There are three things that remain—faith, hope, and love—and the greatest of these is love." (1 Corinthians 13:13 TLB)

June 15

Do you have a secret, My child?

I know every secret in your heart, My precious child. That's because we are connected in a way more profound than words—heart to heart, soul to soul. I hear your prayers, but I also feel what's inside you: your hopes, worries, and even the things you can't put into words. When your heart aches, I think it too. When you're excited or happy, I celebrate with you.

That's why you should never be afraid to come to Me. Please tell me about your troubles, your dreams, and your worries. Even if you don't have the right words, I still understand because I know you well. When you talk to Me, I listen with all My heart and care about everything you're feeling.

No one in the world knows you the way I do. You're never alone because I'm always here, closer than you imagine.

Remember: God knows the inner feelings of your heart and soul.

Bible Treasure: "It is because of this solemn fear of the Lord, which is ever present in our minds, that we work so hard to win others. God knows our hearts, that they are pure in this matter, and I hope that, deep within, you really know it too." (2 Corinthians 5:11 TLB)

June 16

Hello, are you ready to turn impossible into possible, My child?

Dream big, My child—reach for the sky and imagine the most amazing things! You can bring Me your biggest, boldest dreams because I can do far more than you could ever dream up. Your imagination has limits, but I don't. I love working beyond what you think is possible.

So go ahead—dream big, grand, and exciting dreams about who you want to be and what you want to do. I'll help you along the way, but remember, your dreams won't happen without effort. I need you to be ready to work hard, learn, and grow. Maybe you'll need to study at a particular school, train your body, or practice a skill every day. Whatever it takes, I'll be with you every step of the way.

With My help and your effort, even the impossible can become possible. Never stop dreaming, hoping, and trusting in the fantastic things I can do in your life.

Remember: God can work beyond your greatest dreams.

Bible Treasure: "Now glory be to God, who by his mighty power at work within us is able to do far more than we would ever dare to ask or even dream of—infinitely beyond our highest prayers, desires, thoughts, or hopes." (Ephesians 3:20 TLB)

June 17

Is that Jesus standing next to you, My child?

Being a Christian is more than attending church or praying, My precious child. It means following Jesus—the world's Savior—and letting His love shine through you. Being a Christian isn't just a name; it's who you are and how you live. You don't need to tell people you're a Christian—they'll see it in your kindness, love, and how you treat others.

When Jesus lives in your heart, people will notice how you speak and act. Love others the way Jesus did. Be forgiving, even when someone hurts you, because that's what Jesus would do. You show the world who He is when you forgive and love him as He did.

If you do your best to live the way Jesus wants, you'll have a fantastic life filled with joy and purpose. And don't forget—Jesus showed the world what hope looks like by his love.

Remember: Your hope for tomorrow is in your heart today.

Bible Treasure: "He has kept this secret for centuries and generations past, but now at last it has pleased him to tell it... And this is the secret: Christ in your hearts is your only hope of glory." (Colossians 1:26-27 TLB)

June 18

Hello, My Sacred Heart,

Faith is fantastic, isn't it, My lovely child? It's believing in something even when you can't see, hear, taste, touch, or feel it. Faith whispers to your heart that something is true, even when your mind doesn't fully understand it. It takes faith to believe in Me. You can't hear My voice with your ears, yet you talk to Me. You can't see Me with your eyes, yet you read about Me daily in this devotional.

I hope you feel proud of your faith in Me. Some of your friends might think believing in Me is silly or a waste of time, but trust Me—it's never a waste! Your faith grows even more when you follow your heart and soul. The more you pray and read about Me, the more accurate I'll feel to you.

Faith is your superpower, especially when life gets tough. Even if the future seems uncertain, hope and believe that I'll always help you. I'm here, guiding you toward your dreams, even when you can't see the path ahead. Faith and hope always point toward your future; follow them.

Remember: Never give up hope; hope is your connection to the future.

Bible Treasure: "What is faith? It is the confident assurance that something we want is going to happen. It is the certainty that what we hope for is waiting for us, even though we cannot see it up ahead." (Hebrews 11:1 TLB)

June 19

I have a secret,

Do you know what gossip is, My child? Gossip is when people share stories about someone else—stories that may not even be true. It's like a game of telephone: the story starts with one person, but as it's told repeatedly, it changes and grows until it's nothing like the truth. Gossip can hurt and tear people down, and I don't want that for you or anyone else.

When someone brings gossip to you, I want you to pause. Please don't pass it along. Instead, gently remind them not to spread it either. Imagine if the story was about you—how would you feel? Stopping gossip right where it starts is like putting out a spark before it becomes a wildfire.

I created you to spread love, not rumors. Choose kindness and let your words bring life, not harm. Treat others how you want to be treated, and you'll shine My light in a world that needs it.

Remember: Spread God's love, not your friend's gossip.

Bible Treasure: "Anyone who refuses to slander others, does not listen to gossip, and never harms a neighbor." (Psalm 15:3 LTB)

June 20

Listen well, My child!

What should you do if you hear gossip, My child? Gossip is like a spark—it only spreads when you pass it along. It travels through whispers, texts, emails, and posts online. But here's the truth: gossip only keeps going if someone repeats it. You can stop it in its tracks!

When someone brings gossip to you, stand tall and say, "No more gossip!" Imagine stomping your feet to send the message loud and clear. You hold the power to let it end with you. If you don't pass it along, the gossip fizzles out like a flame with no fuel.

Instead of talking about others, why not talk about Me? I love when you share stories about My goodness and how I'm working in your life. Let your words build others up, not tear them down.

My child, you were made to share truth, kindness, and love. Gossip has no place in your heart when you follow My ways.

Remember: Let Gossip die when it meets you. Let My love guide your words!

Bible Treasure: "A gossip goes around spreading rumors, while a trustworthy man tries to quiet them." (Proverbs 11:13 TLB)

June 21

Hello, My Friend maker!

Gossip creates trouble, My child. When you talk about someone behind their back, it doesn't stay a secret for long. Eventually, they'll find out, and that can hurt their feelings. When people are upset with you, it feels heavy. Friendships can break, and bad feelings can grow.

But that's not what I want for you! Instead of spreading gossip, why not talk to the person face to face? You might be surprised by what you discover! Maybe they enjoy the same things you do, like riding bikes, playing games, or drawing. When you take the time to get to know someone, you can make a new friend.

Friendships built on honesty and truth are like strong bridges—they hold up under anything. Gossip and rumors? They're shaky and crumble fast. Choose kindness, My child. Be someone others can trust.

Remember: Spreading truth and love builds stronger friendships than spreading gossip ever could. You can do this—I'm with you every step of the way!

Bible Treasure: "Fire goes out for lack of fuel, and tensions disappear when gossip stops." (Proverbs 26:20 TLB)

June 22

Hello, My superhero!

Yes, My child, even Jesus, was gossiped about. The people of His time were just like people today. Instead of asking Him directly, they whispered behind His back. Instead of seeking the truth, they made things up to satisfy their curiosity. Gossip isn't new—it's been around for a long time.

But you, My precious one, don't have to follow that path. When you hear something about someone, pause. Don't repeat it. Instead, take the brave and kind approach—find out the truth. You don't need to be a detective or a superhero to do this. Just ask the person directly, with a friendly heart and kind words. A simple question can clear up confusion and build understanding.

It might take more effort, but knowing the truth is worth it. When you take time to get to know someone, you might discover a new friend. Living in truth brings peace to your relationships and reflects My love.

Remember: Gossip is old, but kindness and truth are timeless!

Bible Treasure: "They wanted to see Jesus, and as they gossiped in the Temple, they asked each other, 'What do you think? Will he come for the Passover?'" (John 11:56 TLB)

June 23

What the good word, My child?

I want you to stay far away from the Gossip, My child. Did you know it's on the same list as greed, hate, and lying? That's because gossip hurts people, just like those other things do. And I know you don't want to hurt anyone, do you? When you gossip, you're spreading pain instead of My love.

I created you to speak truth and kindness, just like I do. You're walking in My ways when you say honest and uplifting things about others. But when you gossip, you're stepping off the path I've laid for you. Don't worry—I always forgive you when you stumble. But let's work together to stop gossiping, okay? The more you practice, the easier it will be.

You're not alone in this, My precious child. I'm here to help you speak with love, just as I do. Choose your words wisely—they can build or tear others up. Let's use them for good!

Remember: when you choose kindness over gossip, you act like God!

Bible Treasure: Their lives became full of every kind of wickedness and sin, of greed and hate, envy, murder, fighting, lying, bitterness, and gossip." (Romans 1:29 TLB)

June 24

Hello, My good doer!

Gossip is sneaky and brings along other harmful behaviors, my child. Laziness is one of them. When people stop trying to do what's right, they often fall into gossip and other unhealthy habits. Evil actions like these stick together; they can take over your life before long. But I know that's not who you want to be!

It takes effort and discipline to avoid gossip and speak kind, honest words. You must stay alert daily, watching what you say and do. Sometimes, you might slip up—and that's okay. Just come to Me, ask for forgiveness, and keep trying. I'm always here to help you do better.

I remind you about gossip often because it can hurt others deeply, and I want your friendships to grow strong, not fall apart. When you choose kindness over gossip, you show My love to the world. And when you do, you'll find that you keep your friends—and make even more!

Remember: Gossip can ruin a friendship, but love and kindness make friendships last forever.

Bible Treasure: "Yet we hear that some of you are living in laziness, refusing to work, and wasting your time in gossiping." (2 Thessalonians 3:11 TLB)

June 25

Hello, My Sacred Heart!

Do you love going to your friends' houses, My child? Sleepovers are so much fun! You can share pizza, play with toys, read books, and maybe even camp out in sleeping bags on the floor—just like an adventure in the forest. It's an excellent time to laugh and make memories together.

But while enjoying your time, be careful not to gossip about other friends. Gossip can sneak into conversations, but it hurts people and breaks trust. When someone hears you gossip, they might wonder, *Do they talk about me behind my back too?* That can make friendships crumble; I don't want that for you.

Instead, let your sleepovers be full of kindness and fun. Play games, share stories, or even talk about how much I love all of you. If you're ever curious about someone, don't spread rumors—why not call them and ask how they're doing? When you choose truth and love, your friendships grow more substantial.

Remember: Your friends will trust you when your words are kind and genuine. Let love guide your friendships!

Bible Treasure: "Besides, they are likely to be lazy and spend their time gossiping around from house to house, getting into other people's business." (1 Timothy 5:13 TLB)

June 26

Hi there, are you staying safe, My child?

I want you to know something very important. I'll never tempt you to do things that aren't good for you. Temptation is when someone or something tries to pull you into doing something you know isn't right. Sometimes, even your friends might try to get you to join them in making bad choices. But you don't have to follow them. You can stand firm and say, "No, good friends don't lead each other into trouble!"

Whenever you hear a little voice inside urging you to do something, stop and think— "Is this voice kind, helpful, and loving?" If it is, that's Me guiding you! If it's not, don't listen. I'll never tell you to do something hurtful or wrong.

Start your day by praying to Me and filling your mind with good thoughts. When you do, you'll find it's easier to choose good things and stay far away from bad ones. I promise to lead you on the right path every time. Remember, good choices lead to good things, and avoiding temptation keeps your heart safe and happy.

Remember: You've got this! Let's walk together today.

Bible Treasure: *"Don't bring us into temptation, but deliver us from the Evil One."* (Matthew 6:15 TLB)

June 27

Hello, My precious angel!

Did you know I have special messengers called angels? But here's something amazing: not all angels come from heaven. Sometimes, I send people—like your parents, teachers, pastors, or leaders—to bring My messages to you. They might not have wings, but they share My wisdom and love to help guide you. Listen closely when they give you advice; they're like heavenly helpers with lots of earthly experience!

My messengers want to keep you safe and away from trouble. They'll guide you toward making good choices and staying far from temptation. On the other hand, people who choose to do wrong often hang out with others who do the same. That's not where I want you to be. Instead, pray for them. Ask Me to help them, but don't follow their bad example.

Your job is to stay close to the good people I've placed in your life and listen to My messengers. They'll show you the way to stay safe and happy. Remember, I'm always here to guide you, too.

Remember: Pray for evil people, stay with good people.

Bible Treasure: *"I will send my angels, and they will separate out of the Kingdom every temptation and all who are evil."* (Matthew 13:41 TLB)

June 28

Hello, My strong and amazing child!

Did you know you're strong in spirit? Every time you pray, read your Bible, worship Me, and spend time with Christian friends, your spirit becomes even more substantial—just like exercising strengthens your body. Think of these spiritual habits as a workout for your soul! Keep growing and stretching your spiritual muscles every day.

Why is this important? Because when temptation comes—and it will—you'll need to be ready. Sometimes, your body or mind might feel too tired or weak to resist, but your strong spirit can step in and say, "No, I'm choosing what's right!" Remember all the prayers, Bible verses, and lessons you've learned when that happens. They're like tools in your spiritual toolbox, ready to help you stand firm.

Whenever you feel tempted, come to Me in prayer. I'll give you the strength you need. Together, we can overcome anything! With a strong spirit and My help, there's no challenge too big for you.

Remember: You must be strong in body and spirit to resist temptation.

Bible Treasure: *"Keep alert and pray. Otherwise, temptation will overpower you. For the spirit indeed is willing, but how weak the body is!"* (Matthew 26:41 TLB)

June 29

Hello, My brave and wise child!

I'm here to guide you away from every temptation. When you feel tempted to do something wrong, pray to me. Prayer is like a flashlight in the dark—it shows you the way and gives you the strength to make the right choice. Never be afraid to ask for My help. I'm always ready to lead you toward what is good and faithful.

But you're not alone in this journey! I've given you parents, teachers, and other adults who love you and want to help. They're like a team of helpers cheering you on, offering advice and support. Don't try to face temptations yourself— let Me and the people I've placed in your life guide you.

You always have a choice, My child. When you're unsure, pause and seek My help. Talk to those who care about you; together, you'll find the strength to do what's right. Remember, you don't have to face anything alone!

Remember: You have a team of earthly angels waiting to help you.

Bible Treasure: *"Immediately the Holy Spirit urged Jesus into the desert. There, for forty days, alone except for desert animals, he was subjected to Satan's temptations to sin. And afterwards the angels came and cared for him."* (Matthew 1:12-13 TLB)

June 30

Hello, My amazing child!

Let's talk about something important: temptation. Once you give in to it, it gets easier to keep doing the wrong thing. It's like walking down the wrong path—the more you do it, the harder it is to turn back. But you don't want to be stuck on that path, do you?

Here's the good news: prayer is your secret weapon! When you pray and ask for My help, I'll give you the strength to stand tall against temptation. You'll face challenging moments, but remember—I'm always here to guide and protect you.

If something feels wrong or makes you think, "This isn't a good idea," stop! Talk to Me in prayer. Then, reach out to your parents or a trusted adult. Together, we'll help you make the right choice. Overcoming evil starts with asking for help—and I promise, help is always just a prayer away.

Remember: Always seek help when you face temptation.

Bible Treasure: *"There he told them, 'Pray God that you will not be overcome by temptation.'"* (Luke 22:40 TLB)

July 1

Hello, My precious and dearly loved child!

I know you try hard to resist temptation, but sometimes, you might give in no matter how strong you are. Don't worry—you're not alone. Every one of My children faces this. What matters most is what you do next. When you give in to temptation, come to Me immediately and ask for forgiveness. My love for you never changes, and I'm always ready to help you get back on track.

It's also important to ask for forgiveness from anyone you hurt. Temptation doesn't just affect you—it can hurt others, too. For example, taking something that isn't yours can cause someone else to lose what they worked for. If you say unkind words, it might hurt someone's heart deeply.

When you make a mistake, don't let it turn into a habit. Stop, ask for forgiveness, and let Me help you make better choices. I'm here to guide you, no matter what. Please do your best to resist temptation, but always remember, My forgiveness is stronger than any mistake.

Remember: God will always forgive you when you give into temptation.

Bible Treasure: *"For Moses wrote that if a person could be perfectly good and hold out against temptation all his life and never sin once, only then could he be pardoned and saved."* (Romans 10:5 TLB)

July 2

Hello, My Sacred Heart!

Did you know you never face temptation alone? I am always with you, and so is Blessed Jesus, who understands precisely what you're going through. Jesus faced temptations, too—far bigger than anything you'll ever encounter. He was even tempted to deny His connection to Me but resisted every time.

I don't just tell you what to do; I show you! Jesus is your living example of resisting evil and choosing what's right. You can learn so much from His life. Open your Bible to the New Testament and discover the fantastic ways Jesus overcame temptation. Watch how He prayed, trusted Me, and stood firm, even when it was hard.

I know being good all the time isn't easy. I gave you Jesus as a pattern to follow and a plan to succeed. When you choose to live like Him, you're taking steps to resist temptation and grow stronger. And when you pray to Me, I'll give you the help you need for today.

Remember: Jesus showed you how to resist temptation.

Bible Treasure: *"For since he himself has now been through suffering and temptation, he knows what it is like when we suffer and are tempted, and he is wonderfully able to help us."* (Hebrews 2:8 TLB)

July 3

Do you ever worry, My precious child?

Worry feels like carrying a heavy backpack filled with "what ifs" and "what about." Sometimes, you might worry about things that haven't yet happened or not having enough of something you think you need. But let Me tell you a secret: You don't have to carry that heavy load alone.

When you feel worry creeping into your heart, talk to Me. I'm here, ready to listen. Instead of focusing on what feels impossible, trust Me to help you find a way. I see what you're going through and can guide you to the answers you need. I might even send special people to help you along the way. Worry can't solve your problems, but I can!

Faith is like a light that chases away the shadows of worry. Every time you trust Me, your heart will feel a little lighter. I promise I'm always here to help you. You are never alone.

Remember: Faith is an excellent substitute for worry.

Bible Treasure: "So Potiphar gave Joseph the complete administrative responsibility over everything he owned. He hadn't a worry in the world with Joseph there, except to decide what he wanted to eat!" (Genesis 39:6 TLB)

July 4

My precious child, do you know what worry does?

Worry takes a tricky situation and makes it feel even bigger and scarier than it is. Sometimes, when you worry, you might try to handle everything alone, pushing others away or refusing to listen. But guess what? You don't have to do that. You're not alone.

When you feel overwhelmed, talk to someone you trust—like your parents. They love you and want to help. And don't forget, you can always speak to Me! Through prayer, you can tell Me everything in your heart. I've helped many people through various challenges and can help you, too.

Worrying doesn't solve anything. It can make you feel worse—sometimes even sick! I don't want that for you, My child. I want you to feel peace and strength, not fear. When you pray to Me, we can work together to find a solution. Remember, most problems have answers, and I'll guide you toward them. You need to trust Me.

Remember: Share your problems; worry can make you sick.

Bible Treasure: "Stop your anger! Turn off your wrath. Don't fret and worry—it only leads to harm." (Psalm 37:8 TLB)

July 5

Good morning, sleepy head,

My precious child, have you ever spent the night tossing and turning, your mind swirling with thoughts you can't seem to stop? Your worries throw a party in your head when you only want peaceful sleep. But did you know that I never meant for you to carry your fears to bed?

Pillows are for resting, not for solving problems. So, before you close your eyes each night, could you take a moment to talk to Me? Share everything on your mind—every worry, every fear, every "what if." When you say "Amen," you're telling Me you trust I'll take care of it. Let Me handle your troubles so you can enjoy sweet, peaceful dreams.

Sleep is My gift to help you feel strong and ready for a new day. Without it, your mind and body feel tired, making everything seem harder. Trust Me, child, you'll think much more clearly after a good night's rest. So, pray, let go of your worries, and sleep in peace. I'm watching over you. Always.

Remember: If you worry too much, you will sleep very little.

Bible Treasure: "The man who works hard sleeps well whether he eats little or much, but the rich must worry and suffer insomnia." (Ecclesiastes 5:12 TLB)

July 6

Hello, My precious bird lover,

My wonderful child, take a moment to look outside your window. Do you see any birds? Are they reading books, answering emails, or driving buses? Of course not! Birds don't do the things humans do, and they don't waste time worrying like many of my children do.

Birds live each day knowing I'll provide for them. They search My creation for food, trusting their needs will be met. And guess what? You are even more precious to Me than the birds flying in the sky! If I take care of them, don't you think I'll take care of you too?

I know there are times when things feel hard. Maybe your family doesn't have much money, or you're worried about having enough food or clothes. But I've placed people and places in this world to help. Talk to your parents or someone you trust; together, you can find those helping hands. Instead of fretting, look for the ways I've already made a way for you.

Remember: God created the world to support all of life.

Bible Treasure: "Look at the birds! They don't worry about what to eat—they don't need to sow or reap or store up food—for your heavenly Father feeds them. And you are far more valuable to him than they are." (Matthew 6:26 TLB)

July 7

My precious child, do you ever worry about what others are doing?

You may wonder what grade a friend got on a test or worry about what they think or say. But while you're busy focusing on their lives, are you taking care of your own? Sometimes, My children forget to pay attention to their challenges because they're so caught up in someone else's.

I want you to remember that it's okay to focus on yourself first. That's not selfish—it's wise! Imagine trying to see clearly with a big board blocking your view. You must deal with your problems before you can help anyone else with theirs.

Helping others is essential, but you can't give your best to them until your heart and mind are right. So take care of yourself, ask Me for help, and let's work through your challenges together. Once we've done that, you'll be in a better place to help your friends.

Remember: Your problems may be greater than those in your friends' lives.

Bible Treasure: "And why worry about a speck in the eye of a brother when you have a board in your own?" (Matthew 7:3 TLB)

July 8

Hello, My Sacred Heart,

I want you to know something amazing: the same spiritual power I gave to Jesus is here for you, too. You never have to face life alone—I'm always right by your side, walking with you step by step, holding your hand. When worries creep in, or the future seems scary, remember that I'm here, ready to give you strength.

Faith is the key to feeling My presence in your life. Faith is believing in Me and knowing I can help you, love you, and guide you to become the very best version of yourself. When you pray, trust that I hear you. I'll answer in ways that show you My love and care, even when things seem harsh.

So don't give up or let frustration take over. You don't know what's ahead, but I do—and trust Me, wonderful things await you. Stay close to Me, and I'll help you through every challenge, just as I helped Jesus. The best is yet to come, My child.

Remember: You have the same power of the Holy Spirit as Jesus.

Bible Treasure: "Just think how much more surely the blood of Christ will transform our lives and hearts. His sacrifice frees us from the worry of having to obey the old rules and makes us want to serve the living God. For by the help of the eternal Holy Spirit, Christ willingly gave himself to God to die for our sins—he being perfect, without a single sin or fault." (Hebrews 9:14 TLB)

July 9

Hello, My perfect creation!

Hello, My precious one! Close your eyes for a moment. Cover your ears with your hands. What do you see? What do you hear? Nothing, right? That's how it was before I created the world—no sky, sun, moon, singing birds, or barking dogs—just stillness and emptiness.

But then I moved. I spoke! My voice broke through the silence like a song. "Let there be light!" I said, and suddenly, a light appeared, chasing away the darkness. I smiled as I watched light and darkness separate—day and night were born! Before that, everything was a jumbled-up mess, but I brought order and beauty into the chaos.

Do you know what I thought as I created that first day? "This is good!" I loved it. And I made it all for you, My child—to enjoy, explore, and marvel at. Every sunrise and every starlit night whispers My love for you.

So, whenever you look around at the world, remember this: I am the One who made it all just for you. And I am still delighted in my creation, especially you!

Remember: God is the creator of what exists.

Bible Treasure: *"When God began creating the heavens and the earth...Then God said, 'Let there be light,' and light appeared. And God was pleased with it... Together they formed the first day." –*(Genesis 1:1–5 TLB)

July 10

Hello, My busy child!

Did you know there was a time when the sky and the sea didn't exist as you know them? Imagine clouds of hot steam floating around—no kites flying, no swimming in the ocean, just misty vapors everywhere. It was like the steam from a hot shower filling the air. What a mess!

I couldn't leave it like that. So, with My words, I set everything in motion. A mighty wind swirled and spun, lifting the sky high above while the oceans, lakes, and rivers settled below. It was spectacular! I watched joyfully as My creation came together—blue skies stretching wide, waters sparkling in the sunlight.

Even though seeing it was amazing, I knew My work wasn't done yet. Have you considered your homework or chores and thought, "*I still have so much to do*"? That's how I felt. I still had more wonders to create for you, My child.

But remember this: great things take time. Just like I took My time to create the universe, you can take your time to finish what's important, too.

Remember: God had to work for several days to create the universe. Not all things can be completed in a short time.

Bible Treasure: *"And God said, 'Let the vapors separate to form the sky above and the oceans below.' So God made the sky, dividing the vapor above from the water below. This all happened on the second day."* –(Genesis 1:6–8 TLB).

July 11

Hi there, My colorful child,

Did you know there was a time when the world was just water and sky? The blue water and sky were nice, but something was missing—it wasn't colorful or exciting. So I decided to create something new.

First, I gathered the water into big oceans, letting the dry land peek through. Then, I got to work planting every kind of tree, flower, and grow you can imagine. Suddenly, the earth was bursting with color! Green grass, towering trees, bright flowers, and rich fruit all came alive. And I didn't stop there! I made sure the colors would change with the seasons—reds, oranges, yellows, and even snowy whites.

But I didn't just want the plants to look pretty; I made them helpful, too. Trees and plants started producing fruits, nuts, and berries—delicious treats for everyone! I was so happy as I stepped back to admire My work. The world was beginning to look as beautiful as I imagined, just for **you.**

Remember: Every plant and tree on earth came from God.

Bible Treasure: *"Then God said, 'Let the water beneath the sky be gathered into oceans so that the dry land will emerge.' And so it was... Then God said, 'Let the earth burst forth with every sort of grass, seed-bearing plant, and fruit trees.' And God was pleased. This all occurred on the third day."* –(Genesis 1:9–13 TLB)

July 12

Hello, My little star-gazer!

Did you know there was a time when the sky was dark and empty? No sun to brighten your day, no moon to light up your night, and no twinkling stars to make you smile. I decided to change that!

I placed the sun right in the middle of the sky to give light to the earth during the day. Then I set the moon near your world so you'd never face complete darkness at night. But I didn't stop there! I scattered stars all over the heavens like tiny diamonds. When you look up, you see beauty everywhere—and they even help you find your way at night.

Oh, and those seasons you enjoy. They help plants grow, provide food, and make life even more wonderful. I love hearing My children sing about the lights I made, like when you sing *Twinkle, Twinkle, Little Star.*

Remember: Sing to the glory of God's creation.

Bible Treasure: *"Then God said, 'Let bright lights appear in the sky to give light to the earth and to identify the day and the night; they shall bring about the seasons on the earth, and mark the days and years.' And so it was... And God set them in the sky to light the earth. And God was pleased. This all happened on the fourth day."* –(Genesis 1:14–19 TLB).

July 13

Hello, My little adventurer!

Imagine this: the oceans, rivers, and lakes were once quiet, empty waters. The skies above? Silent and still. But I had a plan to fill them with life and excitement.

I became the first-ever "fisherman," but instead of catching fish, I created them! I made tiny guppies, shimmering schools of fish, and enormous whales. Soon, the waters were alive with all kinds of creatures swimming and playing. Even baby sharks joined the fun!

Then, I turned My attention to the skies. I created birds with colorful feathers that could flap, fly, and chirp. Some made nests in trees, and soon, baby birds hatched from eggs. The once-empty air was now filled with flapping wings and joyful songs.

Remember when I told you how the sky and ocean started as a messy vapor? They were bursting with life, and I was so happy to see it all! Everything was perfect for My creation—just as I imagined it.

Next time you hear birds chirp or watch fish swim, remember: I made them all to fill the world with life and beauty just for you.

Remember: God filled the waters and the air with life.

Bible Treasure: *"Then God said, 'Let the waters teem with fish and other life, and let the skies be filled with birds of every kind.' So God created great sea animals, and every sort of fish and every kind of bird. And God looked at them with pleasure and blessed them all. 'Multiply and stock the oceans,' he told them, and to the birds he said, 'Let your numbers increase. Fill the earth!' That ended the fifth day."* –(Genesis 1:20–23 TLB)

July 14

Hi, My curious friend!

Can you imagine a world with just fish in the water and birds in the sky? I loved the fish and birds I had made, but something was missing. The earth needed life—creatures that could run, jump, crawl, and roam.

So, I thought about all the animals I could create. Then, with the words "Let there be," they came to life just as I imagined! Elephants with long trunks, giraffes with tall necks, playful puppies, and curious kitties appeared. Kangaroos hopped, monkeys swung from tree branches, hippos splashed in the water, and snakes slithered through the grass. Everywhere I looked, the earth was bursting with life and movement.

It made Me so happy to see the animals enjoying the world I made for them. But even with all the fantastic creatures filling the earth, something was still missing—something very special. Do you know what it could be? Stay tuned!

Remember: God created every animal; take care of them as if they are your pets.

Bible Treasure: *"And God said, 'Let the earth bring forth every kind of animal—cattle and reptiles and wildlife of every kind.' And so it was. God made all sorts of wild animals and cattle and reptiles. And God was pleased with what he had done." –* (Genesis 1:24–25 TLB).

July 15

You Are My Special Creation!

Do you know what was missing from My amazing world? Someone like Me! I wanted someone who could think, care, and create like me. So, I made something very special—you!

When I created humans, I didn't make them look like Me, but I gave them My heart for creation. I wanted boys and girls to love, care for, and take care of everything I made. I also allowed them to create new things, just like Me!

Let's try something together: imagine a cute little kitten in your mind. Now, grab a piece of paper and draw it. See? You just created something from your imagination! That's part of what makes you unique—you are a creator, too, just like Me.

But being like Me also means caring for what you create and what I've given you. Whether it's your drawing, your pets, or the world around you, you can nurture and protect it. Isn't that amazing?

Remember: God made you to create things.

Bible Treasure: *"Then God said, 'Let us make a man— someone like ourselves, to be the master of all life upon the earth and in the skies and in the seas.' So God made man like his Maker. Like God did God make man; Man and maid did he make them."* – (Genesis 1:26–27 TLB)

July 16

Hello, My Sacred Heart!

After I finished creating the world—the sun, moon, stars, animals, plants, and even you—I decided to stop. Not because I was tired but because I was filled with joy! Everything was perfect, and I wanted to celebrate and enjoy what I had made.

So, I created the Sabbath, a special day of rest and remembering. This day is holy, a time for you to pause and appreciate all the wonderful things I've given you. It's also a day to enjoy your life and the fantastic things you can do.

On the Sabbath, I hope you'll worship Me with your prayers, sing songs, go to church, and spend time with the people you love. I also want you to know that I celebrate *you* on this day! You are a very special part of My creation, My beautiful child and I delight in you.

Remember: God gave you a day to rest and to worship.

Bible Treasure: *"Now at last the heavens and earth were successfully completed, with all that they contained. So on the seventh day, having finished his task, God ceased from this work he had been doing, and God blessed the seventh day and declared it holy, because it was the day when he ceased this work of creation."* – (Genesis 2:1–3 TLB).

July 17

You are My number 1!

Did you know that I am all you'll ever need? I love you more than anyone and want to be the most important part of your life. But sometimes, My children forget about Me.

Some think their toys or games are more important. Others get so busy with fun and entertainment that they forget to pray or talk to Me. And some have stopped thinking about Me altogether. That makes My heart so sad because I love them so much.

Please don't forget about Me, My child. I hope you'll always keep Me as number one in your life. When you talk to Me and pray, you'll feel My love growing in your heart. I can help you more than anyone else ever could.

When something or someone becomes more important to you than Me, it's like making them your god. But remember, I made you, love you, and always be here for you. Keep Me first; I'll fill your life with joy and love.

Remember: God should always be number one in your life.

Bible Treasure: *"I am Jehovah your God who liberated you from your slavery in Egypt. 3 You may worship no other god than me."* (Exodus 20:2-3 TLB)

July 18

Hello, My beloved child!

Did you know that sometimes things can sneak in and take My place in your heart? It's true! Some of My children spend so much time and energy on things like video games that they forget all about Me. Games are fun, but they become like a little god when they rule your life.

I don't want anything to replace Me—not games, statues, or beautiful paintings or symbols. None of those things can love you back or answer your prayers. I am the only one who can fill your heart with the love you need. I love you with a big love that will never run out or grow cold.

Spend time with Me, My child. Talk to Me in your prayers, sing songs, and share My love with others. When you keep Me first, your life will be joyful, and you'll always feel My love.

Remember: Love God with all your heart, and give yourself to God completely.

Bible Treasure: *"You shall not make yourselves any idols: no images of animals, birds, or fish. You must never bow or worship it in any way; for I, the Lord your God, am very possessive. I will not share your affection with any other god!"* (Exodus 20:4–5 TLB)

July 19

Do you like your name, My child?

Did you know that My name is very holy? It's so unique that I want you to use it only for good things. When you pray to Me or ask for My help, you're using My name in a way that makes Me happy. But some of My children use My name to say hurtful or naughty things, which makes Me so sad. I would never speak badly about anyone, and I hope you won't either.

Always use kind and respectful words when talking about Me. I always think the best thoughts about you, and I was hoping you could do the same for others.

And here's something important to remember: don't make promises and swear by My name. If you make a promise, keep it because it's the right thing to do—not because you brought Me into it. Instead, pray to Me for help keeping your commitments, and I'll be beside you.

I love hearing you speak My name in prayers, songs, and blessings. Use My name to spread love and kindness, and I'll always be proud of you.

Remember: God has a holy name; only use it well.

Bible Treasure: *"You shall not use the name of Jehovah your God irreverently, nor use it to swear to a falsehood. You will not escape punishment if you do."* (Exodus 20:7 TLB)

July 20

Happy Sunday, My child!!

Did you know that the Sabbath, or Sunday for you, is a gift from Me? It's a day of blessing—a special time to rest, relax, and honor Me. I don't want you to think of it as a chore or something you must do. The Sabbath is a chance for you to enjoy the life I've given you and act like Me!

Remember when I told you I made you in My image? You don't look like Me, but you can act like Me. When you rest on the Sabbath, you're following My example. After I created the world, I rested—not because I was tired, but because I wanted to enjoy everything I had made. You can do the same.

The Sabbath is also a day for your family to come together. Your parents work so hard, and this is a time for all of you to rest, worship, and enjoy each other.

So take this day as My gift to you. Rest, relax, and honor Me. I made this day just for you, My child because I love you.

Remember: The Sabbath is the day you are to act like God by resting.

Bible Treasure: *"Remember to observe the Sabbath as a holy day. Six days a week are for your daily duties and your regular work, but the seventh day is a day of Sabbath rest before the Lord your God... For in six days the Lord made the heaven, earth, and sea, and everything in them, and rested the seventh day; so he blessed the Sabbath day and set it aside for rest."* (Exodus 20:8–11 TLB)

July 21

Hello, My grateful child!

Did you know your parents are a special gift from Me? I chose them to care for, love, and guide you as you grow. From the moment you entered this world, your parents have worked hard to care for you. They fed you, bathed you, rocked you to sleep, and changed all those diapers (and there were a lot!).

As you got older, they sent you to school so you could learn and become the amazing person you're meant to be. They work daily to ensure you have clothes, food, and everything else you need. They do it because they love you—just like I love you.

One of the best ways to honor your parents is by saying "thank you" for everything they do. Helping with chores, being kind, and listening to them are great ways to show love and appreciation.

Your parents love you so much because they are My children too. I hope you'll always cherish them and grow to understand how special they are.

Remember: Be thankful to your parents for everything they do for you.

Bible Treasure: *"Honor your father and mother, that you may have a long, good life in the land the Lord your God will give you."* (Exodus 20:12 TLB)

July 22

Hello, My lively child!

I know you would never think of hurting someone, but I want to talk to you about something very serious—taking another person's life. When someone commits murder, they end their life forever. That life can't come back, and many people are heartbroken. Parents lose their children, children lose their parents, and husbands or wives lose their partners. It's a pain that changes lives.

I gave the commandment, "You must not murder," so everyone knows how precious life is. All life belongs to Me—every breath you take and every beat of your heart is a gift from Me. That's why treating everyone with kindness, love, and respect is so important.

If you ever feel angry, remember there's always a way to solve problems without hurting anyone. Anger can lead to bad decisions, but you can choose peace. I believe in you, My child.

Show others the love and care you want for yourself. Life is a beautiful gift, and I want you to celebrate and protect it.

Remember: Treat everyone with kindness and love.

Bible Treasure: *"You must not murder."* (Exodus 20:13 TLB)

July 23

Hello, My faithful child!

Did you know that when people get married, they promise to love and care for each other forever? A family usually starts with a mom and dad who work together to raise their children with love and kindness. It takes teamwork and love to keep a family firm and happy.

When a mom or dad falls in love with someone other than their husband or wife, it can cause big problems. I know this may be a little hard to understand right now, but when someone breaks that promise of love, it can hurt the whole family. Marriages can fall apart, and it's especially hard for the children.

That's why I gave the commandment only to love the person you're married to. Marriage is a beautiful gift, and when both people work together to make each other happy, it helps the family grow strong and full of love.

One day, if you get married, remember to treasure that person and the family you create. Love deeply and be faithful, just like I am always faithful.

Remember: You can't be married to one person and love another person. too

Bible Treasure: *"You must not commit adultery."* (Exodus 20:14 TLB)

July 24

Hello, My trusty child!

Isn't walking through a store and seeing so many amazing things exciting? Maybe you've wished you could take whatever you wanted. But that's not how life works. Everything you see was made or raised by someone who worked hard to create it. When their product is sold, they earn money to care for their family and buy the necessary things.

When someone steals, it hurts the person who made that product. Their hard work is taken away, and they can't provide for their loved ones. That's why stealing is wrong— it takes what doesn't belong to you and harms someone else's dreams and needs.

I want all My children to have enough to eat, wear good clothes, and live happy lives. When you respect what belongs to others and work hard for what you need, you're helping Me make that possible for everyone.

Remember: When you steal, you hurt the person who made the product.

Bible Treasure: *"You must not steal."* (Exodus 20:15 TLB)

July 25

Hello, My honest child!

Do you know why it's so important to tell the truth? Because when you lie, you stop acting like Me. I created you in My image, hoping you could try your best to act as I would. Sometimes, it can be challenging, but following My way is always the best choice.

When you tell a lie, you create something that isn't true. I only create truth. If you tell too many lies, you'll need more to cover up the first ones. Before long, your life could feel like a tangled web of untruths. And when people discover your lies, they may stop trusting you. Even your friends might worry you'll tell lies about them, and they may not want to be around you anymore.

Lies don't belong in the world I created and shouldn't be part of your world either. I will always be honest with you, My child, so you can trust everything I say. And I want you to be truthful so that others can trust you.

Remember: Lies are not part of the world I created.

Bible Treasure: *"You must not lie."* (Exodus 20:16 TLB)

July 26

Hello, My Sacred Heart!

Have you ever seen something your friend has and thought, "*Wow, I wish that was mine!*"? It's fun to play with your friend's toys or visit their house but remember; those things belong to them, not to you.

Sometimes, wanting what someone else has can turn into envy. Envy can make you feel unhappy, and before long, you might start to dislike your friend just because you think their things are better than yours. But guess what? Your friends might look at your stuff and feel the same about what you have!

Enjoy the wonderful things you've been given—they are probably gifts from people who love you. Instead of feeling envious, be thankful for what you have and happy for what your friends have. Sharing your toys and playing with theirs makes time together so much more fun.

Envy only makes you feel bad and keeps you from enjoying the blessings already in your life. So, let's focus on gratitude and kindness instead!

Remember: What you have is a gift from a loving person.

Bible Treasure: *"You must not be envious of your neighbor's house, or want to sleep with his wife, or want to own his slaves, oxen, donkeys, or anything else he has."* (Exodus 20:17 TLB)

July 27

Hello, My blessed child!

Did you know there's a special spiritual gift waiting inside you? That's right—I placed it there just for you! Each of My children has unique gifts that I carefully selected. These gifts are like tools to help you serve others and improve the world.

You may wonder why I gave different gifts to different people. It's because one person alone can't do everything! That's why I chose many of My children, including you, to be My servants in different ways. But there's one thing all My children share: the ability and courage to praise the name of Jesus.

When you talk about Jesus and show others His love, you let the world know you belong to Me. Never hesitate to proclaim His name. I've given you the power to speak about Him with joy and confidence so others can see that I live in you.

You are My unique child, and your gift is essential. Use it to serve, love, and let the world know that Jesus is Lord!

Remember: The Holy Spirit gives you the power to proclaim the name of Jesus.

Bible Treasure: *"But now you are meeting people who claim to speak messages from the Spirit of God. How can you know whether they are really inspired by God or whether they are fakes? Here is the test: no one speaking by the power of the Spirit of God can curse Jesus, and no one can say, 'Jesus is Lord,' and really mean it, unless the Holy Spirit is helping him."* (1 Corinthians 12:3–4 TLB)

July 28

Hello, My gifted child!

I have something very important to ask you—will you be My helper? The world is full of people who need My love, and My church needs many hands to serve others. I need you!

Can you sing in the choir to bring joy through music? Could you help at church school or pass out bulletins on Sunday morning? Maybe you can share stories about Me with people who haven't heard about My love yet. Whatever your gift, there's a way for you to help.

Don't worry if you don't know how to do everything yet. Grown-ups will teach you, and I will guide you every step of the way. I've given you unique gifts; when you use them, others will see My power shining through you.

Everyone has different talents, but I work through all of My children. When we all work together, amazing things happen! The love and kindness you share will help build My church and bring joy to everyone.

Remember: You display the power of God when you serve the people of God.

Bible Treasure: *"Now God gives us many kinds of special abilities, but it is the same Holy Spirit who is the source of them all. There are different kinds of service to God, but it is the same Lord we are serving... The Holy Spirit displays God's power through each of us as a means of helping the entire church."* (1 Corinthians 12:4–7 TLB)

July 29

Hello, My helpful child!

Did you know I've given you special spiritual gifts? That's right—they come from Me, the Holy Spirit, and are just for you. You may not know your gifts yet, but don't worry. I will show you when the time is right.

These gifts aren't just for you to enjoy—they're meant to help and serve the people around you. When you use your gifts wisely, you're making your community a better place. Imagine a world where all My children work together, helping one another. Isn't that beautiful?

The best way to discover and use your gifts is to stay connected to Me. Talk to Me every day in prayer, and I will guide you. For now, practice being kind and good to everyone you meet—a gift I want all My children to share.

Your spiritual gifts are My unique way of showing how much I love you and how much you can help others. I can't wait to see you use them!

Remember: Spiritual gifts are gifts from the Holy Spirit.

Bible Treasure: *"To one person the Spirit gives the ability to give wise advice; someone else may be especially good at studying and teaching, and this is his gift from the same Spirit... He gives power for doing miracles to some, and to others power to prophesy and preach."* (1 Corinthians 12:8–10 TLB)

GREED

THOUGH HE
AS ALWAYS
GREEDY, NOW
HE HAS NOAM
NE HAS NOTHING;

OF OF ALL THE
HE DREAMED:
THINGS HE DREAMED
----- NONE REMAIN."
– JOB 20:20 TLB

July 30

Hello, My generous child!

Let's talk about something important: greed. Greed is when you want everything for yourself and don't want to share it with anyone. Imagine not letting friends play with your toys, not sharing your candy, or not letting others join your group of friends. That's what greed does—it keeps you from sharing and making new friends.

Greedy people are always wanting more, but the truth is, they'll never have enough to make them happy. They may work hard to collect everything they desire, but in the end, they can't keep any of it forever. Someone else will eventually own the things they spent their whole lives trying to gather.

I want you to be different. Be like Me—I share! I share My creation, the air you breathe, the food you eat, and the clothes you wear. If I didn't share, there wouldn't be anything for you or anyone else.

Practice generosity, My child. Share your things, your time, and your love with others. You'll find that the more you share, the more friends you'll have—and friends are worth more than anything else!

Remember: Greed is always wanting more than you can ever have.

Bible Treasure: *"Though he was always greedy, now he has nothing; of all the things he dreamed of—none remain."* (Job 20:20 TLB)

August 1

Hello, My happy heart!

Imagine a world where no one shared anything. You call to order a pizza, but the pizza guy says, "No, these pizzas are mine!" You save up to buy a shiny new bike, but the salesperson says, "Nope, I'm keeping this bike for myself." Life would become tough and lonely, wouldn't it?

I love to give, and I encourage you to share, too. When you share, it's a sign that I'm working in your heart. Greedy people don't listen to Me and miss out on the joy of helping others. A generous heart, on the other hand, brings happiness—to you and to the people you help!

It takes hard work to earn money and buy the things you need, but generosity doesn't just mean giving money. You can also share your time, talents, or even a kind word. Before long, you'll discover that giving is fun! And one day, you'll feel the joy of someone being generous to you in return.

Remember: Generosity always feels better than greed.

Bible Treasure: *"The lazy man longs for many things, but his hands refuse to work. He is greedy to get, while the godly love to give!"* (Proverbs 21:25–26 TLB)

August 2

Hello, My thoughtful child!

I'm so glad you take care of your body. Showering, brushing your teeth, eating healthy foods, exercising, and sleeping well are all important. These things keep you strong and make you look great. But did you know there's another part of you that needs care, too? It's the part inside you—your heart and mind.

Imagine this: you look nice outside, but if you act greedy or mean, people won't want to be around you for long. The truth is what's inside your heart always comes out. Your words and actions show people what you're thinking and feeling. If your heart is full of kindness, love, and generosity, that's what others will see. But if it's full of selfishness or mean thoughts, people will notice that, too.

That's why it's so important to take care of the "inner you." Think good thoughts, be generous, and speak kindly about others. When you care for your heart and mind, you'll shine on the inside and the outside!

Remember: What you think on the inside will soon be known by people on the outside.

Bible Treasure: *"Then Jesus said to him, 'You Pharisees wash the outside, but inside you are still dirty—full of greed and wickedness!'"* (Luke 11:39 TLB)

August 3

Hello, My beautiful child!

Have you ever filled a bucket with water and dirt? Maybe you stirred it with a stick and watched as the water turned into muddy goop. Imagine putting a big scoop of your favorite ice cream into that muddy bucket and eating it. Yuck! That doesn't sound very tasty.

Your life is like a bucket I gave you to keep clean and holy. When you think evil thoughts, say mean things, or act unkindly, it's like filling your bucket with mud. If you keep adding bad things, your life becomes a messy mix that doesn't look or feel good.

But when you fill your life bucket with kindness, love, and prayer, it becomes something beautiful and good. Be kind to others, talk to Me daily, read your Bible, and help people whenever possible. If you do these things, your life will stay clean, and you'll feel My blessings pouring into your bucket.

Let's keep your bucket full of the good things I've given you so your life can be a blessing to others.

Remember: Fill your life with goodness, and you will create a good life.

Bible Treasure: *"Their lives became full of every kind of wickedness and sin, of greed and hate, envy, murder, fighting, lying, bitterness, and gossip."* (Romans 1:29 TLB)

August 4

Follow Me, My child!

Have you ever played "Follow the Leader"? It's a fun game where you copy someone's moves, trying to do everything they do. But let Me tell you something important—not everyone you follow will lead you to a safe or happy place.

Some of My children don't follow Me because they hold on too tightly to the things of this world. When you clench your fists to hang onto your possessions, it's hard to open your heart to Me. Greedy people trust only what they can keep for themselves. Their hearts stay closed, and that makes Me so sad. I want all My children to love Me as much as I love them.

When you trust Me, you'll see that I provide everything you truly need. It's okay to enjoy the things you have, but always place Me first in your life. Open your heart to My love, and I will fill your life with blessings greater than anything you could hold in your hands.

Follow Me, My child, and I'll lead you to joy, peace, and love like you've never known before.

Remember: God should be more important than anything or anyone else in your life.

Bible Treasure: *"You can be sure of this: The Kingdom of Christ and of God will never belong to anyone who is impure or greedy, for a greedy person is really an idol worshiper—he loves and worships the good things of this life more than God."* (Ephesians 5:5 TLB)

August 5

Hello, are you ready to follow the leader?

Have you ever noticed the leaders in your church? Many have special training and spend time teaching others how to live a life full of love and joy with Me. They generously give their time, talents, and treasures to help others and strengthen their community. They are shining examples of what it means to live a life that honors Me.

You can follow their example! Even if you don't have money to give, you can donate your time by helping around the church. You can also give something very special—your prayers. When you talk to Me, don't just pray for yourself. Ask Me to bless your church leaders and others in your community. Praying for someone is one of the kindest and most generous gifts you can give.

Generosity works like a ripple in a pond. When you share what you have—time, love, or prayers—it grows and spreads, blessing others in ways you can't imagine. So, follow the example of generous leaders and let your kindness shine!

Remember: Follow generous leaders and practice sharing what you have.

Bible Treasure: *"The deacons must be the same sort of good, steady men as the pastors. They must not be heavy drinkers and must not be greedy for money."* (1 Timothy 3:8 TLB)

August 6

Hello, My Sacred Heart!

Have you ever known someone who seems trapped by their greed? Greedy people often find themselves alone because they love things and money more than they love others. Their greed acts like an invisible jail, keeping them from making friends or sharing love. Seeing any of My children stuck in such a place makes my heart so sad.

But here's the good news: escaping that invisible jail is easy! All you have to do is love people more than things. When you care for others like I do, you'll naturally make friends who want to spend time, laugh, and play with you.

If you know someone who struggles with greed, pray for them. They need your love and help to see how wonderful life can be when they let go of greed and hold onto love. You have the power to show them a better way.

Always remember that you can change the outcome of tomorrow by choosing to act differently today. Be generous and loving, and watch how your kindness spreads to those around you!

Remember: We can change greed into love by acting generously.

Bible Treasure: *"These teachers, in their greed, will tell you anything to get hold of your money. But God condemned them long ago and their destruction is on the way."* (2 Peter 2:3 TLB)

August 7

Hi, My generous child!

I want to share something special with you today. Giving is one of the most wonderful things you can do! When you give, you share joy, love, and kindness with others—guess what? Giving makes you a happier person, too!

I am a giver. I give sunshine and rain so crops can grow, filling plates with delicious food. I created playful fish in the sea and loving pets like dogs and cats just for you. I gave you tall, sturdy trees to climb and cool shade on warm, sunny days. Every beautiful thing you see is My gift to you.

When you notice all these blessings, it fills your heart with gratitude. And when you share My blessings—whether it's a smile, a helping hand, or something you treasure—you're being like Me. You're bringing joy to others and spreading My love in the world.

Go ahead, My generous child. Give someone a kind word, a wave, or a hug today. Watch how it lights up their heart and yours, too!

Remember: You can bless people and bring them joy.

Bible Treasure: "*She decided to return to Israel with her daughters-in-law, for she had heard that the Lord had blessed his people by giving them good crops again.*" (Ruth 1:6-7 TLB)

August 8

Hello, My patient child!

I love blessing My children with what they need, often when they need it most. But sometimes, waiting can feel so hard, can't it? Some of My children get so anxious that they pace around or fidget, thinking it will make things happen faster. Trust Me—running in circles won't bring your blessings any quicker.

Instead of worrying, talk to Me. Pray. Remember how I told you that prayer isn't just about asking for things? It's a way to stay close and connected to Me. When you're connected to Me, you'll follow Me more closely and notice all the good things I'm doing in your life.

Too many of My children miss the blessings I send because they're too distracted or impatient to see them. Don't let that be you. Stay alert, keep praying, and watch closely—I send you new blessings every day.

Remember: Look for the daily blessings that come from God.

Bible Treasure: *"Pour out your unfailing love on those who know you! Never stop giving your blessings to those who long to do your will."* (Psalm 36:10 TLB)

August 9

Hello, let me see your thankful heart!

It's Me, the Holy Spirit, and I want to tell you something that fills My heart with joy: hearing you say, "Thank you." When you thank Me, it shows you've noticed the blessings and gifts I sent you. It's like a beautiful song to My ears, especially when an entire church joins to thank Me. That kind of praise fills My heart with happiness!

When you give thanks, it tells Me two important things. First, it shows that you saw and received My blessing. Second, it reminds you that I always keep My promises to take care of you. I want everything you need to be happy, healthy, and loved. Those are my gifts to you every single day.

When you thank Me for the joy in your life, your health, and the love you feel, it's the greatest compliment you can give Me. And you can be sure—I'll keep working to bring those blessings to you because I love you so much.

Remember: Giving thanks to God allows you to see what God has done in your life.

Bible Treasure: *"I face your Temple as I worship, giving thanks to you for all your loving-kindness and your faithfulness, for your promises are backed by all the honor of your name."* (Psalm 138:2 TLB)

August 10

You may not know it, My little one, but your strength comes from Me. I give you the strength you need to keep your body healthy so you can run and jump and do all the things you like to do. You receive strength for your body from the sun I created. The sun gives you energy by supplying vitamins for your body. You also receive energy from the sun by eating the plants and animals that grew in sunlight. The sun is significant to all of My creation and is vital for your existence.

I also supply the power and spiritual energy you need to stay connected to Me. By reading devotions, reading from your Bible, going to church, and praying, you receive strength for your spirit or soul. All of the resources I mentioned come from Me, or I inspired other people to write about Me.

These are just a few of the examples of how I give and bless you each day. I love to provide you with the things you need to keep you strong.

Remember
Your strength comes from God.

When I pray, you answer me and encourage me by **giving** me the strength I need. (Psalm 138:3 TLB)

August 10

Hello, My strong child!

You are stronger than you know because your strength comes from Me! I give you the energy you need to run, jump, and enjoy all the fun things you love to do.

Did you know the sun I created helps keep you strong? Its light gives your body energy by providing vitamins, and it helps grow the plants and animals you eat. Without sunlight, life wouldn't be the same. The sun is one of My amazing gifts, shining brightly for all My creation.

But there's more! I also give you spiritual strength. You strengthen your spirit when you read devotions like this, spend time with your Bible, go to church, or pray. These things keep you connected to Me, and I inspire them all because I love you.

I bless you daily with what you need to stay strong—in your body and heart. You are My precious child, and I delight in giving you the strength to live and grow.

Remember: Your strength comes from God.

Bible Treasure: *"When I pray, you answer me and encourage me by giving me the strength I need."* (Psalm 138:3 TLB)

August 11

Hi there, My forgiven child!

I want to tell you about one of My greatest gifts— forgiveness. Sin is what separates us. When you choose to do bad things, you turn away from Me, making it harder for you to hear My voice. But when you follow Me and My ways, we stay close, and I can bless you with all you need.

Here's the wonderful part: even if you mess up (and everyone does), I am always ready to forgive you! That's why Jesus came—to ensure you can always be free from sin. You never have to be afraid to ask for My forgiveness. Just say, "Please forgive me in Jesus' name," and I will forgive you completely. Your sins will disappear, and you'll feel brand new inside.

This is the power of My love and grace, and I delight in sharing it with you. Forgiveness is My gift to you, and it's always waiting whenever you need it. You are My beloved child, and nothing makes Me happier than giving you new life through My love.

Remember: God loves to forgive you.

Bible Treasure: *"For the power of the life-giving Spirit—and this power is mine through Christ Jesus—has freed me from the vicious circle of sin and death."* (Romans 8:2 TLB)

August 12

Hello, I have a great gift for you, My child.

I want you to know something very special—I am the greatest gift you will ever have. I know you better than anyone else because I created you. I am the one who gives your life every single day.

Do you remember Adam, the very first person I made? He started as a lifeless form shaped from the red dust of the earth. Then I breathed My Spirit into him, and he came to life—a living, breathing person like you!

Now try this: hold your hand under your nose and breathe out. Feel that rush of air? That's Me! I am the breath in your body, the Life-Breath that gives you energy for today and hope for tomorrow. I am always with you, giving you guidance, direction, and strength.

I gave your life, My child, and I sustain it every day. Stay close to Me, and remember that I am the greatest gift you'll ever have. I love you so much and will always be with you.

Remember: You will have no greater gift than the Spirit of God.

Bible Treasure: *"The Scriptures tell us that the first man, Adam, was given a natural, human body but Christ is more than that, for he was life-giving Spirit."* (1 Corinthians 15:45 TLB)

August 13

Hello, My Birthday Child,

Do you love when your house is filled with laughter and love on your birthday? It's so much fun. Balloons floating, your favorite meal on the table, and a cake piled high with candles—one for each year of your fantastic life. When you blow out those candles, I'm smiling at you and celebrating the wonderful person you're becoming.

Your home is more than just walls and a roof. It's a treasure chest of memories! Birthday parties, graduations, even little moments like snuggling under a blanket during a storm. It's where you grow, laugh, and love. And guess what? I'm always there, too. You don't have to look far to find Me— I'm in the joy of your family, the quiet of your prayers, and every corner of your home.

So, enjoy your home. Fill it with kindness, love, and laughter. When you need to talk, I'm ready to listen. You're never alone because My Spirit makes your house peaceful and joyful.

Remember: A home is a place to find God and family.

Bible Treasure: *"Every year when Job's sons had birthdays, they invited their brothers and sisters to their homes for a celebration. On these occasions, they would eat and drink with great merriment." (Job 1:4 GNT)*

August 14

Hello, My Happy One,

Did you know your home is one of My favorite places to be? Your home isn't just where you live—I live with you! I love being part of your life, whether you're playing games, helping with chores, or even just laughing with your family. Amazing things can happen when you invite Me into all the little moments.

When I'm in your home, joy spreads like sunshine, even on cloudy days. I hear every prayer you whisper and answer them at just the right time. My blessings fill your home with peace, kindness, and love—like little gifts everyone can feel. And even when you don't always see eye to eye with your siblings, My joy can help bring you back together.

So, remember to make room for Me in everything you do. When I'm in your home, it becomes a place where laughter rings, love grows, and happiness improves every day.

Remember: God can fill your home with happiness.

Bible Treasure: *"If you were pure and good, he would hear your prayer and answer you and bless you with a happy home."* *(Job 8:6 GNT)*

August 15

Hi, My Growing Child,

Did you know I gave you your home as a special place to grow, laugh, and feel loved? Your parents work hard to care for you and provide everything you need to grow strong and healthy. And if you have siblings, they're there to share love, laughter, and sometimes even a little silliness! But remember, no two homes are precisely the same. Some have two parents, some don't. Some have brothers and sisters, and some don't. No matter what, your home is where you'll learn and grow.

Here's something amazing: you can help make your home even better! You can keep your room neat, thank your parents, and pitch in with chores like taking out the trash or helping with dishes. Your kindness and hard work bring joy and comfort to everyone in your home.

When your family works together, your house becomes a place full of love, peace, and teamwork. Remember, you have an important role in making your home happy!

Remember: Try to be as helpful as possible around your home.

Bible Treasure: *"When Joseph awoke, he did as the angel commanded and brought Mary home to be his wife." (Matthew 1:24 TLB)*

August 16

Hello, can you make room for Jesus?

Did you know Jesus has no home unless you give Him one? That's right—your heart and home are where Jesus wants to stay! Every time you talk to Me in prayer or read your devotional, you're making space for Him. Maybe you've seen a picture of Jesus in your home, or you wear something special that reminds you of Him. However, living like Him is the most important way to invite Jesus in.

Do you remember what Jesus taught you? Love everyone, just like He loves you. It's not always easy, but when you forgive someone who's hurt you, say "thank you" to someone kind, or show love even when it's hard, you're making room for Jesus. He'll bring peace and joy to your home when you let Him in.

Your home is a special place; it can be even more amazing when Jesus is part of it. Make room for Him in your heart and in how you treat your family every single day.

Remember: Jesus wants to be part of your home; invite him in.

Bible Treasure: *"But Jesus said, 'Foxes have dens and birds have nests, but I, the Messiah, have no home of my own—no place to lay my head.'" (Matthew 8:20 TLB)*

August 17

Hello, Jesus is ready to move in,

Do you know your home is the perfect place to practice what you learn at church? Church is where you hear about Jesus and learn all about Me, but your home is where you live out your faith daily. It's like putting your lessons into action!

Your Bible is like a unique instruction book for living as one of My children. It teaches you how to pray, love, and live like Jesus. You can practice by reading the Bible daily, praying at meals to thank Me for your food, or even filling your home with Christian music. These little things make your home feel like a place where Jesus lives with you.

You'll feel closer to Me when you practice being a Christian at home. You'll grow in your faith and shine My love in your family. So, every day, try to live like Jesus is right there with you—because He is!

Remember: Practice what you learn in church at home.

Bible Treasure: *"And every day, in the Temple and in their home Bible classes, they continued to teach and preach that Jesus is the Messiah." (Acts 5:42 TLB)*

August 18

Hello, have you seen Me in Church?

Do you know how much I love you and everything I've created? When someone hurts one of My children, it makes My heart ache. I feel the pain of the hurt and the sadness of the one who caused the harm. That's why I want you to be kind and careful with others—because when you love each other, you're showing love to Me, too.

I also live in My churches, where My children come together to worship Me. Just like your family works hard to take care of your home, My family—the church's people—cares for My house. They clean, repair, and make it beautiful so it's a special place for everyone to feel My presence.

If someone damages My church, whether they realize it or not, it saddens Me deeply. I want you to pray for them, My child. Pray they see how much I love them and want their heart to be a home for Me, too.

Remember: God lives in all the places of worship; take good care of your church.

Bible Treasure: *"If anyone defiles and spoils God's home, God will destroy him. For God's home is holy and clean, and you are that home." (1 Corinthians 3:17 TLB)*

August 19

Hello, My Sacred Heart,

Did you know I have a beautiful home in heaven waiting for all My children? It's a place where love and joy fill every corner. When someone you love has died, they've come to be with Me. I was there when they were born, walked beside them their whole life, and welcomed them home when their time on earth was done.

I can't fully explain how wonderful heaven is, but I can tell you this: no one feels pain, sadness, or loneliness there. Instead of roofs over their heads, My love surrounds and protects everyone forever. There's no hunger because I fill their hearts with love and joy. Imagine a place where everyone is always happy, healthy, and close to Me—heaven!

But don't worry, My child; I want you to enjoy every moment of your life here. Live happily, love deeply, and shine brightly for Me. Your heavenly home will be ready for you when the time comes.

Remember: God lives in the home where people go after they die. Heaven is God's glorious home.

Bible Treasure: *"And quite obviously when they talked like that, they were looking forward to their real home in heaven."* *(Hebrews 11:14 TLB)*

August 20

Do you like rainbows, My child?

Aren't rainbows amazing? After a big rainstorm, when the air is fresh, and the world feels brand new, the sunlight shines through tiny drops of water, and suddenly—a dazzling rainbow stretches across the sky! It's like a beautiful hug for the earth. But did you know that rainbows aren't just pretty to look at? They're My special promise to you.

A long time ago, I placed rainbows in the sky as a reminder of My promise: I will never again destroy the earth because of sin. There are still storms and challenging times, but I don't send them to harm My creation. Instead of destruction, I chose forgiveness. Through the life, death, and resurrection of Jesus, I gave you a way to receive My grace and love.

The next time you see a rainbow, remember this: I love you more than you can imagine, and I'll always keep My promise to take care of you and the world around you.

Remember: The rainbow signifies God's promise to love you.

Bible Treasure: *"I have placed my rainbow in the clouds as a sign of my promise until the end of time, to you and to all the earth." (Genesis 9:13 TLB)*

August 21

Hello, My Wonderful Child,

Have you ever made a promise to your friends? Maybe you promised to share your favorite toy or help them with something important. When you keep your promises, your friends know they can trust you. But if you break your promises, they might stop believing what you say. That's why keeping your word is so important—it shows others they can count on you.

Sometimes, My children make promises to Me. They tell Me they'll do better, love more, or follow My ways. But sometimes, they forget their promises and go back to living as if they never made them. Do you know what I do? I listen carefully to their promises and step in to help them keep their word. I know when your heart is sincere, and I'll guide you to find a way to fulfill what you've said.

So, the next time you make a promise, to Me or anyone else, remember: I'm here to help you follow through. You can count on Me, and I love it when you try to do what you've promised!

Remember God will always help you fulfill your promises.

Bible Treasure *"But Abram replied, 'I have solemnly promised Jehovah, the supreme God, Creator of heaven and earth.'" (Genesis 14:22 TLB)*

August 22

I have a promise for you, My Precious Child,

Do you know how many promises I've made to My children over the years? Each one was special and filled with love. Remember the rainbow? It's My promise never to flood the earth again. I promised Abraham he would become the father of a great nation. I led the children of Israel out of slavery in Egypt because I promised them. And I sent Jesus to show My love and offer forgiveness for everyone's sins.

Now, I have a promise just for you. I promise to love you forever. That might sound simple, but it's the most significant promise. No matter where you go, how old you grow, or what you do, My love will never leave you. I'll never break this promise or change My mind—it's forever.

When you love someone, you give them a piece of your heart, and that's precisely what I've done for you. My love is My greatest gift and yours to keep forever.

Remember: God will always love you; that is a promise.

Bible Treasure: *"And now I have heard the groanings of the people of Israel, in slavery now to the Egyptians, and I remember my promise." (Exodus 6:5 TLB)*

August 23

Hello, My Pinky Child,

Have you ever made a pinky swear with a friend? You hook your little fingers together and promise to keep a secret or follow through on something important. You trust your friend to keep their promise, but sometimes, people break promises, don't they? When that happens, it can make it harder to trust them again.

But let Me tell you something amazing: when I make a promise, it's unbreakable. My promises are holy, sacred, and full of truth. I never lie, and I never fail to keep My word. When I make a promise to My children, it becomes a foundation they can always stand on.

Some people swear on a Bible when making a promise because they know it represents My truth. But My promises are even more powerful than that—they are as holy as I am. You can trust Me completely, My dear child, because I will never disappoint you.

Remember: God's promises are as holy as God.

Bible Treasure: *"The Lord's promise is sure. He speaks no careless word; all he says is purest truth, like silver seven times refined." (Psalm 12:6 TL*

August 24

The wait is over. My child,

Do you know how special it is to wait for a promise? Imagine your friend promises to come over tomorrow for a playdate. You wait all day, excited, wondering if they'll keep their word. If they forget, it can feel disappointing, right?

But here's something amazing about Me: I never forget My promises, and I always keep them. My promises are like the sunrise—you can count on them daily. When I make a promise, it's more than words—it's a sacred, unbreakable truth. I will always do what I say, My child.

So, when you're waiting for one of My promises to come true, trust that My timing is perfect. Whether it happens today, tomorrow, or years from now, it will happen because I love you, and My word never fails. You can always count on Me, forever and ever.

Remember: God always remembers all promises.

Bible Treasure: *"For every promise from God shall surely come true." (Luke 1:37 TLB)*

August 25

Do you remember your baptism, My child?

Did you know that I am fulfilling a promise made a long, long time ago? Back then, people worshipped Me, sang songs about Me, and prayed to Me, but only a few knew Me as the living God who could be part of their daily lives. I felt far away from many of My children.

But everything changed with Jesus. After Easter, when Jesus rose from the grave, My promise to be close to everyone became real. It started on Pentecost—the birthday of the Christian church—when I filled the hearts of Jesus' followers with My holy presence. And I still do that today!

I come to you in your baptism. Baptism is a special moment when My promise to always be with you is fulfilled. That day, I entered your life and made your heart My home. From that moment, I've been with you, closer than anyone or anything, loving you from the inside out.

You, My child, are proof of My promise. I came to you at your baptism and will never leave you.

Remember: God's promise was fulfilled in you at your baptism.

Bible Treasure: *"In one of these meetings, he told them not to leave Jerusalem until the Holy Spirit came upon them in fulfillment of the Father's promise, a matter he had previously discussed with them." (Acts 1:4 TLB)*

August 26

Hello, My Sacred Heart,

Long ago, I made a fantastic promise and sent prophets to share it with the world. These prophets told My children that a day was coming when everyone would know Me and feel My love in their hearts. Their words were written down in the Hebrew Scriptures, or the Old Testament, so My promise would never be forgotten.

Then, something incredible happened—My promise came true! The New Testament tells the story of how Jesus fulfilled My promise. He brought salvation, saved everyone from sin, and allowed you to live forever with Me in heaven. Can you imagine? My love is so big that I created a way for you to be with Me, not just now, but forever.

These promises of forgiveness and eternal life are the greatest gifts I could ever give. They are My way of saying, "I love you, and I want to be with you always."

Remember: The prophets told the people about the love and forgiveness Jesus would bring.

Bible Treasure: *"This Good News was promised long ago by God's prophets in the Old Testament." (Romans 1:2 TLB)*

August 27

Hello, I am thankful for you, My child,

Did you know it's hard to see all the help you get each day if you think you're doing everything independently? Humble people understand that life is a team effort. Your teacher helps you learn at school. Maybe your parents or siblings help with homework. The bus driver or your parents will take you to and from school. The kitchen staff prepares your lunch, and the custodian keeps your school clean. So many people are working together to make your day go smoothly!

Being humble means noticing and appreciating the help you get. It's about saying "thank you" and understanding that we all need one another. Humble people don't think they have to do everything alone—they know life is better when we help each other.

And guess what? I'm part of your team, too! I'm always beside you, helping you reach your goals and cheering you on. It's My most incredible joy to help you, and I hope you're thankful for all the ways I work in your life.

Remember: A humble person knows there are people to help them.

Bible Treasure: *"Humble men are very fortunate!" he told them, " for the Kingdom of Heaven is given to them. Those who mourn are fortunate! for they shall be comforted." (Matthew 5:3-4 TLB)*

August 28

Hello, My magnetic Child,

Have you ever met someone who demands help by yelling or stomping their feet? Maybe they expect everyone to stop what they're doing and focus on their needs right away. It's exhausting. People can get tired of helping someone who acts that way, and eventually, they might stop helping altogether.

But let Me tell you a little secret: kindness changes everything. When you ask for help politely and with a thankful heart, people are happy to help you. It feels good to help someone who appreciates it. Demanding attitudes push people away, but kindness and humility attract helpers like a magnet.

When you think you're above others and act like everyone owes you something, you'll quickly find that isn't true. But when you remember you're equal to all My children and treat others with respect, people will gladly come to your aid. So, be kind, My child, and always say "thank you" when someone lends a hand.

Remember: People don't have to help you; be thankful when they do.

Bible Treasure: *"The meek and lowly are fortunate! for the whole wide world belongs to them." (Matthew 5:5 TLB)*

August 29

Hello, My Just Child,

Do you ever feel like you want everything you see? Every toy on the shelf or every treat you can imagine? It's easy to want more and more, but here's the tricky part: when you always want something new, you forget to enjoy what you already have. Those toys you loved before might get pushed aside, and you'll always look for the next thing.

Instead of wanting more, I want to teach you something amazing: justice. A just person isn't focused on getting more for themselves. They think about others, too. They want everyone to be treated fairly and are happy to share what they have. When you share with others, you bring joy—not just to them but to yourself, too.

A just and reasonable heart is always satisfied. It doesn't need more because it's full of love and kindness. So, My child, instead of longing for more things, try sharing what you have and caring for those around you. That's the kind of joy that lasts forever.

Remember: Justice tries to include people who are left out.

Bible Treasure: *"Happy are those who long to be just and good, for they shall be completely satisfied." (Matthew 5:6 TLB)*

August 30

Try to be, My Merciful Child,

Do you know what it means to be merciful? Mercy shows kindness and forgiveness to someone, even when they might not deserve it. When you are merciful, you don't hold onto grudges when someone says or does something that hurts you. Instead, you let it go, forgive them, and move forward with a heart whole of peace.

I show mercy to My children all the time. When they make mistakes or commit sins, I forgive them when they come to Me in prayer. Mercy brings happiness—not just to the person you forgive, but to you, too! Letting go of hurt means leaving bad feelings behind and focusing on joyful things again.

Being merciful takes courage and strength. It's not always easy to forgive and forget, but when you do, you open your heart to new, happy memories. Mercy helps you grow into the loving, kind person I know you can be.

Remember: Merciful people learn to forgive and forget when someone insults or offends them.

Bible Treasure: *"Happy are the kind and merciful, for they shall be shown mercy." (Matthew 5:7 TLB)*

August 31

Stay Happy if you want to see Me, My child,

Did you know that keeping your heart pure means staying close to Me? I see how hard it is to do good and make wise choices. Keep praying to Me daily, reading your Bible or devotionals, and attending church or Church School. These things help you stay close to Me and far away from trouble.

It's easy to get distracted by other things, like games, toys, or hobbies. Those things are fun, but if you make them the most important thing in your life, everything else—even Me—can seem less important. I want to be number one in your heart, not because I want to take away your fun, but because staying close to Me fills your life with joy, peace, and love.

You can still do what you love—play games, spend time with friends, and enjoy your favorite hobbies. Just make sure you're spending time with Me, too! When I'm first in your life, your heart stays pure, and we'll both be very happy.

Remember: God must be first in your life if you are to remain pure in your heart.

Bible Treasure: *"Happy are those whose hearts are pure, for they shall see God." (Matthew 5:8 TLB)*

September 1

Hello, My Child of Peace,

Did you know I already consider you My son or daughter? That's right—you are one of My beloved children! And do you know how you can show the world that you belong to Me? By being a child of peace.

A child of peace is kind to others, working to bring people together instead of dividing them. That means no name-calling or teasing—those things often lead to hurt feelings or even fights. Instead, try to build friendships by being kind and understanding. A peaceful heart helps others feel loved and included.

But here's a secret: to share peace, you must first find it in your own life. Peace comes when you love Me with all your heart, love others the way I love them, and practice forgiveness and mercy. It might seem like a lot to remember, but it's worth it. Peace brings joy and makes life so much brighter for you and everyone around you.

Remember: You must work for peace, but the result is far better than conflict.

Bible Treasure: *"Happy are those who strive for peace—they shall be called the sons of God." (Matthew 5:9 TLB)*

September 2

Hello, My Faithful Child,

Do you ever feel teased or left out because of your faith in Me? Maybe other children don't understand why you read your Bible or go to church, and they say hurtful things. They might think you're weak or need extra help to handle life's challenges. But here's the truth: everyone needs My help, even those who tease you.

I want you to know that your kindness and strong faith will shine brighter than their words. One day, those same children might come to you for advice or want to learn more about Me. They might even ask to join you at church!

So, be proud of your faith and the life we share. Let your faith be an example of love, strength, and joy. When others see how happy you are with Me, they might decide to follow Me, too. Imagine the joy we could all share!

Remember: Your faith is a living example of what it means to follow God.

Bible Treasure: *"Happy are those who are persecuted because they are good, for the Kingdom of Heaven is theirs." (Matthew 5:10 TLB)*

September 3

Hello, My Sacred Heart,

Do you ever feel worried or upset about the things happening around you? Maybe someone has been unkind, said hurtful things, or even lied about you. It's hard. But let Me remind you of something very special: I'm always with you, and My love for you never ends.

Some people don't understand what it means to be loved by Me. They might tease you or disrespect you because of your faith. But you know better, don't you? You know, My love is forever. You know I keep My promises and fill your life with blessings daily.

When life feels tough, hold onto your faith in Me. It's the most precious gift you'll ever have. Your faith will guide you, comfort you, and one day lead you to your true home in My Kingdom. So, don't let today's troubles get you down. I have an incredible reward waiting for you in heaven.

Remember: Living in God's holy love is a promise that will last forever.

Bible Treasure: *"When you are reviled and persecuted and lied about because you are my followers—wonderful! Be happy about it! Be very glad! for a tremendous reward awaits you up in heaven. And remember, the ancient prophets were persecuted too." (Matthew 5:11-12 TLB)*

JUSTICE MUST PREVAIL. THAT IS THE ONLY WAY YOU YOU WILL BE SUCCESSFUL IN THE LAND THAT THE LORD YOUR LORD YOU GIVING YOU

— DEUERONOMY 16:20 —

September 4

Hello, My Just Child,

Do you know what it means to live a just life? Justice is about treating people fairly and kindly, regardless of how they look, speak, or act. When you live with justice, you respect everyone and care about their feelings and needs. Sometimes, treating people fairly means helping them in ways that are a little different from how you help others. That's okay—justice is about doing what's right for each person.

Sadly, some of My children are mistreated. Maybe you've seen someone left out or disrespected because of the color of their skin, the way they speak, or even how they look. That breaks My heart, My child. I love every one of My children deeply, and I want you to love them, too.

When you meet someone new, try to see them through My eyes. Look for the reasons I love them, just like I love you. Living a just life brings fairness, kindness, and love into the world.

Remember: God loves everyone as much as God loves you.

Bible Treasure: *"Justice must prevail. That is the only way you will be successful in the land that the Lord your God is giving you." (Deuteronomy 16:20 TLB)*

September 5

Hello, My Brave Child,

Do you know how powerful you are? Even though you're young, you can stand up for what's right and speak out against what's wrong. You can make a difference when you see something unfair, like bullying or name-calling. If someone is being hurt or teased, don't try to fight back yourself—instead, find an adult who can help.

It's never okay for someone to be called nasty names or mistreated because of the color of their skin, the way they speak, or how they look. You can help by speaking up and refusing to accept those hurtful actions. The world becomes a better, kinder place when people stop tolerating mean behavior.

Justice is about helping everyone feel safe and loved. You can create a place where kindness and fairness rule, where no one has to be afraid of being teased or left out. By standing up for what's right, you're helping to build a world filled with love.

Remember: Justice demands fair and loving treatment for everyone.

Bible Treasure: *"And in your majesty go on to victory, defending truth, humility, and justice. Go forth to awe-inspiring deeds!" (Psalm 45:4 TLB)*

September 6

Hello, are you ready to change your world?

Do you know you have the power to make the world a better place? Treating everyone fairly, honestly, and with kindness creates a just and loving world around you. Not everyone will act the same way, but the people close to you will notice and start treating others like you do. You can build a small group where everyone cares for and respects one another.

If you want to change the world, it starts with you. People often respond to you the way you treat them. When you show fairness, kindness, and respect, they'll likely treat you the same way. That's why it's important to always be on your best behavior—you're also setting the tone for how others act.

Let justice begin with you, My lovely child. Your good deeds will inspire others to follow; before you know it, you'll help make the world brighter and kinder for everyone.

Remember: You are responsible for the justice around you.

Bible Treasure: *"Justice goes before him to make a pathway for his steps." (Psalm 35:14 TLB)*

September 7

When someone wrongs you, it's time for forgiveness, My Child,

Did you know there are many rules to help keep people safe and treated fairly? Some rules are written in holy books, like the Bible, while others are laws created by countries and communities. These rules exist to protect people and make sure no one is mistreated. When everyone follows the rules, life is better and safer for everyone.

But sometimes, people don't follow the rules. When that happens, forgiveness becomes part of justice. If everyone got in big trouble every time they made a mistake, many people would end up in the principal's office, paying fines, or worse! That's why forgiveness is so important.

Jesus taught us to forgive and to try our best not to sin again. You won't always get it right, but that's okay. When you make a mistake, I am here to forgive you and help you do better. You are loved, My child, no matter what.

Remember: God forgives us when we make mistakes and sin.

Bible Treasure: *"For Moses gave us only the Law with its rigid demands and merciless justice, while Jesus Christ brought us loving forgiveness as well." (John 1:17 TLB)*

September 8

Hello, My Loving Child

Do you ever feel like someone is being unfair or unkind to you? Maybe a classmate teases you or says mean things. It hurts. When that happens, teasing them back or getting angry might feel tempting. But let Me tell you something important: fighting back with unkind words or actions won't fix the situation—it only worsens it.

Instead, try something different. Love them, even when they're mean. That's hard to do, but you can pray for them instead of yelling at them. If you feel sad or upset, come to Me. I'll give you the strength you need to stay calm and assertive.

Remember, I am the ultimate judge. I see everything, and I'm working to help those who are mean and unfair, just like I care for you. Trust Me, My child, and know I'm always here to protect and guide you.

Remember: God is our ultimate judge in life.

Bible Treasure: *"For we know him who said, 'Justice belongs to me; I will repay them'; who also said, 'The Lord himself will handle these cases.'" (Hebrews 10:30 TLB)*

September 9

Hello, My Sacred Heart,

Did you know that My love for you is perfect? It's true! My love never gets tired, and it never runs out—not even when My children are mean or forget about Me. I never give up on anyone, and I always want the best for all of My children.

I don't play favorites. My love is perfect because I love each of you as if you were My only child. That means every single one of My children has My undivided attention daily. I hear your prayers, guide you through life, and help you when things get complicated. A love that only works sometimes could never do all that!

I hope you know how deeply I love you, My child. My perfect love is why I can be just and fair with everyone. Remember, I judge with fairness, but I always love first.

Remember: God judges perfectly, but first, God loves with perfection.

Bible Treasure: *"And remember that your heavenly Father to whom you pray has no favorites when he judges. He will judge you with perfect justice for everything you do; so act in reverent fear of him from now on until you get to heaven." (1 Peter 1:17 TLB)*

September 10

Nighttime can feel scary sometimes, can't it, My child?

Shadows seem bigger, noises louder, and your imagination might run wild. But guess what? I'm always right here with you! When the darkness feels too big, talk to Me. Instead of imagining something hiding under your bed, imagine Me standing guard, watching over you as you sleep. I never leave you—not for one second.

When you feel afraid, remember: I am real and with you every night of your life. Talk to Me. Tell Me your fears, and I will bring My peace to your heart. Peace isn't about everything being perfect—it's about knowing I've got you, even when things feel scary or uncertain.

Even grown-ups forget this sometimes. They imagine things about others that aren't true, turning neighbors into enemies. But loving others, even those who seem hard to love, fills their hearts with My peace, too.

Remember: Peace comes when we trust in God to protect us.

Bible Treasure: *"Then I lay down and slept in peace and woke up safely, for the Lord was watching over me." (Psalm 3:5 TLB)*

September 11

Every day, My child, you have a choice—to hold onto peace or let it slip away.

Sometimes, your siblings test your patience, or a friend might say something hurtful. Maybe you didn't do as well as you wanted on a test, and now you feel frustrated. Life can throw many challenges, trying to steal your peace and joy.

But here's the secret: peace starts in your heart. It can't grow in a place filled with anger, frustration, or unkindness. So, when things go wrong, don't focus on what's bad—look for the good. Think about what makes you smile, the blessings you already have, and how much I love you.

Want to feel more peace? Please share it! Do something kind for someone else. Help a friend, forgive a sibling, or say something loving. The more good you do, the more peace you'll find in your heart. Peace isn't just something you feel—it's something you give.

Remember: Peace follows good works.

Bible Treasure: *"Turn from all known sin and spend your time in doing good. Try to live in peace with everyone; work hard at it." (Psalm 43:14 TLB)*

September 12

You don't have to like everyone, but you do have to love them, My child.

Maybe someone said something mean, or you don't click with certain people. But here's a secret: the closer you are to Me, the easier it is to love everyone—even those you think you don't like.

How can you grow closer to Me? Start by talking to Me in prayer every day. Read your Bible and devotionals to learn more about My love. Sing songs that remind you how much I care for you. And don't forget to pray for those you struggle to like—it's hard to hold onto dislike when you bring someone into My light.

When My love fills your heart, something amazing happens: it spills onto others. You'll feel closer to them, even those who seem difficult to love. Remember, it's you who decides how to think about someone. But with My love in your heart, loving others becomes so much easier—and so much better.

Remember: Love comes from God.

Bible Treasure: *"When a man is trying to please God, God makes even his worst enemies to be at peace with him."* *(Proverbs 16:7 TLB)*

September 13

Hello, My Prince of Peace,

That's because He brought a new way to find peace. Jesus showed everyone how to love Me with all their minds, hearts, and souls. He taught that loving Me isn't something you do halfway—it's something you do with all your strength, every part of who you are. That's how much I love you—with everything I am.

Jesus also taught people to love their neighbors as they love themselves. Imagine that! When you love Me, love yourself, and love others, you leave no space for hate to grow. That's how peace is planted in the world—one heart at a time.

When you love like Jesus, you're not just any child. You become a prince or princess of peace! So go ahead, My little peacemaker—love as Jesus loved, and watch the world around you grow brighter and more peaceful.

Remember: You can be a prince or princess when you love as Jesus loved.

Bible Treasure: *"For unto us a child is born; unto us a son is given; and the government shall be upon his shoulder. These will be his royal titles: 'Wonderful,' 'Counselor,' 'The Mighty God,' 'The Everlasting Father,' 'The Prince of Peace.'" (Isaiah 9:6 TLB)*

September 14

Hello, My Peacemaker,

It's like a beautiful garden—everyone has to plant seeds of kindness for it to grow. But if you're angry, calling people names, or even thinking unkind thoughts about someone, it's hard to build that peaceful garden I want for all My children.

I've chosen you to be a little peacemaker today! That means you get to lead others to peace by the way you live. Speak kindly, even when it's hard. Never hurt or harm anyone, no matter how you feel. Show love by doing good to those around you, even to people you don't get along with. And here's a unique challenge: pray for the ones you don't like until you start to love them. I know that's not always easy, but you can do it because I believe in you.

Think about being a peacemaker every day. When you fill your mind with peace and kindness, your actions will follow. And when you lead with peace, others will follow you, too.

Remember: You can be a child that leads adults to peace.

Bible Treasure: *"In that day the wolf and the lamb will lie down together, and the leopard and goats will be at peace. Calves and fat cattle will be safe among lions, and a little child shall lead them all." (Isaiah 11:6 TLB)*

September 15

Hello, My child, I have a gift for you.

When He told His disciples about His death on the cross, He wanted them to know something very important—no matter what happened, He would never be separated from God. Jesus wanted His friends to understand that even though hard times were coming, their faith would carry them through and bring them peace.

And here's the best part: Jesus promised to send Me, the Holy Spirit, to live in everyone who follows Him. That means I'm always with you, right here in your heart, ready to guide, comfort, and help you find peace—even when life feels hard.

I know life can be tricky sometimes. Maybe you're worried about something or feeling sad. When those moments come, talk to Me. Pray and share what's on your heart. If you listen closely, you'll hear My voice, and I'll fill you with the peace you need to keep going.

Remember: God is here to bring peace to you in difficult times.

Bible Treasure: *"I have told you all this so that you will have peace of heart and mind. Here on earth you will have many trials and sorrows; but cheer up, for I have overcome the world."* (John 16:33 TLB)

September 16

Hello, My Sacred Heart,

These life lessons aren't just suggestions—they are My perfect guide to help you do the right thing. When people work together, treat each other kindly, and try their best to get along, peace will bloom in their community like a beautiful garden.

I know it's not always easy to follow Me. Sometimes, you might feel angry, sad, or frustrated with someone. Those feelings are normal, but they're only temporary. Don't let them grow into something bigger, like hate. Instead, remember that peace begins with you. When you fill your heart with peace, it will spill out to everyone around you.

Peace is My gift to you, but I also want you to share it. Together, you and I can create peace in your life, your home, and even the whole world. Let's start today with one peaceful thought, kind word, and loving action at a time.

Remember: Peace is a gift from God you must share.

Bible Treasure: *"But there will be glory and honor and peace from God for all who obey him, whether they are Jews or Gentiles." (Romans 2:10 TLB)*

September 17

What do you need, My precious one?

I want to give you everything you need for this amazing life I've planned for you! But here's something important to understand: giving you everything you *need* isn't the same as giving you everything you *want*. Needs are the things that help you grow strong and happy—like good food, warm clothes, learning at school, a loving family, and friends who care about you. Needs also include your church, your time with Me in prayer, and reading My Word in the Bible.

Wants, though, are a little different. They're things you might desire, like new toys, video games, or other fun stuff. I love it when you enjoy good things, but not everything you want will truly help you. That's why I make sure your needs are met first. You can always trust Me to take care of you, My child.

I delight in your joy and want you to have fun while you grow! Just remember, My most incredible gift to you is the love and care you'll always have from Me.

Remember: God will give you what you need, but not always what you want.

Bible Treasure: *Because the Lord is my Shepherd, I have everything I need!* (Psalm 23:1 TLB)

September 18

Hey there, come rest with Me!

Isn't it the best feeling to sit in the shade of a big tree after running and playing in the sun? The cool breeze on your face, the soft grass under you—it's like your own little slice of heaven.

That's how I want you to feel when you spend time with Me. Imagine sitting beside a peaceful stream, dipping your toes into the cool, sparkling water. Can you feel how refreshing that is? That's what prayer, Bible reading, and listening to My voice can do for your heart and soul. When life feels busy, or you're a little worn out, come rest with Me. Let Me refresh you, like the cool shade on a hot day or the gentle stream that soothes your feet.

You're never too busy to take a moment to be with Me, My child. I'm always here, ready to fill your heart with peace and joy. Rest in My love, and you'll be more assertive and happier daily.

Remember: Time spent with God is like sitting in the shade of a tree beside a cool stream.

Bible Treasure: *He lets me rest in the meadow grass and leads me beside the quiet streams.* (Psalm 23:2 TLB)

September 19

Hello, My strong child,

I love it when you spend time with Me. When you come to Me, it's not just about sharing your prayers or telling Me about your day—though I love hearing all about it! Our time together is also a chance for Me to make your spirit stronger and fill your heart with My love.

I need strong and brave friends like you to share My message with others. Not everyone knows Me the way you do, and that's why you're so special! When you tell people about our friendship and how much I love them, you honor Me. It's simple. Just let them know I care about them and want to be their friend, too.

Don't worry if it feels like a big job—I'll give you all the spiritual strength you need to make a difference. Together, we can show the world how amazing My love is!

Remember: God gives you spiritual strength to share the message of love.

Bible Treasure: *He gives me new strength. He helps me do what honors him the most.* (Psalm 23:3 TLB)

September 20

Never be afraid, My dear child,

Fear not, even when you don't understand something new. It's okay to feel cautious—that's just your heart telling you to take a moment to learn and think before you leap. Being careful is smart and helps keep you safe from harm, especially when trying something for the first time.

But don't let the unknown hold you back. Your faith and trust in Me are like a bright light guiding you through the shadows. You don't need to fear the dark or the unknown because I'm always with you. I will give you the strength and protection you need, no matter what.

When you trust Me, even the scariest shadows fade away. I am right here, holding your hand, guiding you step by step. My love will always keep you safe and show you the way.

Remember: Your faith in God will show you the way in scary times.

Bible Treasure: *Even when walking through the dark valley of death I will not be afraid, for you are close beside me, guarding, guiding all the way.* (Psalm 23:4 TLB)

September 21

Have you ever been on a picnic, My child?

Aren't picnics fun? You can run and play while the food gets ready, then sit outside in the sunshine and enjoy a yummy feast. And the best part? No dishes to wash when it's all done!

Guess what? I love to have picnics with you, too. Imagine being the special guest at a big, joyful picnic where everyone celebrates you—like it's your birthday! There's laughter, singing, and gifts; all your friends are there to make the day even better.

But here's a little challenge: what if you invited someone you don't know well—or even someone you don't like— to your picnic? That sounds hard, but it's the best way to turn an enemy into a friend. When you share kindness, even with those who are hard to love, you share My love with them. That's how friendships grow, My child—with understanding, kindness, and a little courage.

Remember: Enemies become friends when you take the time to know them.

Bible Treasure: *You provide delicious food for me in the presence of my enemies.* (Psalm 23:5 TLB)

September 22

I have a blessing for you, My Special One!

Every day can feel as unique as a birthday picnic, My lovely child! Start your day with a cheerful "good morning" prayer to Me, and I'll be right there with you, ready to make you feel like the most honored guest.

All day long, I'll surprise you with wonderful gifts—blessings from My heart to yours. These blessings are everywhere! The delicious food you eat, the hugs and love from your family and friends, the warm clothes that keep you cozy in the cold, and even My help when things feel challenging or frustrating.

I give you so many gifts that you couldn't hold them all in your arms. My love and blessings for you will always overflow, filling your life with joy and goodness. Every day is a new chance to discover how much I love you, My precious child. So look for those blessings, and let them remind you that I'm always with you.

Remember: God blesses you each day with many great gifts.

Bible Treasure: *You have welcomed me as your guest; blessings overflow!* (Psalm 23:5 TLB)

September 23

Be My BFF, My Sacred Heart!

Our friendship will last forever, My lovely child. I am the breath in your lungs, the One who fills your heart with life, and I will always be with you—now and for all eternity. I know forever is a big idea, but it's true! You started your journey with Me, and one day, after a long and beautiful life, you'll continue it with Me in heaven.

But don't worry My child—you have so much time ahead to laugh, play, and enjoy the love of your family and friends. For now, live each day to the fullest, knowing that heaven is waiting for you. When the time comes, you'll join Me in My glorious home, surrounded by everyone who loves Me, too.

I've prepared the most amazing place for you, where we'll never be apart again. It's filled with joy, love, and My never-ending kindness. Until then, I'm here with you, guiding you and blessing your life.

Remember: You will join God in heaven and live forever in a glorious home.

Bible Treasure: *Your goodness and unfailing kindness shall be with me all of my life, and afterwards I will live with you forever in your home.* (Psalm 23:6 TLB)

September 24

Hello, My lovely one.

Sometimes, when you make a mistake, you might feel a heavy, uncomfortable feeling called shame. That's Me, gently nudging your heart to recognize something wrong. I gave you this feeling to help you learn and grow, so don't fear it. Instead, let it guide you to make better choices next time.

When you feel shame or guilt, it's like a little whisper saying, "You can do better." Listen closely to that whisper, My child, because I want the best for you. I know you don't like feeling bad—nobody does! But remember, shame isn't here to punish you. It's here to teach you.

One of the most powerful ways to release shame is to say, "I'm sorry." When you apologize for your mistakes, it's like clearing away the clouds so the sun can shine on your heart again. I'm always here, ready to help you start fresh.

Remember: Shame is a feeling that keeps you from doing bad things again.

Bible Treasure: *"And cried out, 'O my God, I am ashamed; I blush to lift up my face to you, for our sins are piled higher than our heads and our guilt is as boundless as the heavens.'"* *(Ezra 9:6 TLB)*

September 25

I am very proud of you, My glorious child,

When you follow Me, you walk on a path filled with light, love, and joy. Stay close to Me, and you'll never need to feel ashamed. I'm here to lead you to a life of goodness that shines so brightly that others will see how amazing life with Me can be!

Here's how to stay close: read your Bible, come to church, and talk to Me in prayer daily. These simple things help you grow stronger, kinder, and full of love. When you live this way, you create a life you can be proud of—one that honors Me.

Do you remember how special it is to be one of My disciples? That means the way you live shows others what I'm like. You're showing the world who I am when you're kind, honest, and loving. So, choose good words, make good choices, and know I'm watching with so much pride in My heart. You are My lovely child, and I am so proud of you!

Remember: God is proud of you; keep up the good behavior.

Bible Treasure: *"Help me to love your every wish; then I will never have to be ashamed of myself." (Psalm 119:80 TLB)*

September 26

Hello, My shining light,

I want you to know something very special—I want the absolute best for you and all My children. When people see how you live, I want them to see kindness, love, and joy shining from you. Living in a way that reflects My divine love makes the world brighter and happier.

You can do so much good by working together with others! Helping people, sharing food, and being kind to one another spreads peace and harmony. Whenever you show love, speak kind words or lend a helping hand, you show others what it means to belong to Me. My face lights up with pride when I see you doing these things!

You are My treasure, and your kindness reveals My love in your heart. So, keep sharing that love with everyone around you. Be proud to be one of My precious children because I am so proud of you!

Remember: God is proud of you when you love.

Bible Treasure: *"That is why the Lord who redeemed Abraham says: 'My people will no longer pale with fear or be ashamed.'" (Isaiah 29:22 TLB)*

September 27

Be proud of who you are in Me, My child.

I want you to know something truly amazing—I hope you're never ashamed of the Good News. Do you know what the Good News is? It's this: Jesus gave His life to forgive your sins, and I live in you as a unique, divine gift. The Good News is for everyone, and anyone who accepts it becomes part of My family forever!

Think of it like the most wonderful invitation ever sent. The Good News is My way of inviting everyone to know Me, walk with Me, and one day live with Me in heaven. This invitation is filled with My love and will never expire!

You can help share this incredible message with your friends. Maybe they've never heard about My love, forgiveness, or the promise of eternal life. You could be the one to tell them! So, never feel shy or embarrassed about sharing the Good News. My invitation is for everyone, and I'm so proud when you help others hear about it.

Remember: The Good News is God's invitation to become part of the Christian family.

Bible Treasure: *"For I am not ashamed of this Good News about Christ. It is God's powerful method of bringing all who believe it to heaven. This message was preached first to the Jews alone, but now everyone is invited to come to God in this same way." (Romans 1:16 TLB)*

September 28

You are doing a great job, My child!

You are doing a fantastic job, and I can't tell you how proud I am of you. "What am I doing?" you might wonder. Well, let Me tell you! Whenever you're kind to your family, you do My work. When you help someone, you're working for Me. And when you brighten someone's bad day with a kind word, you're one of My special servants.

Do you know the secret to doing My work? It's simple: love people first. When you fill your heart with love, the right words and actions will follow. Being kind, polite, and friendly is always a win; people genuinely appreciate it. No one likes a bully, but everyone loves someone who's kind. And guess what? Life is much more fun when surrounded by friends who enjoy being around you.

Now, I don't give out gold stars or prizes, but trust Me— your kindness earns something even better: lots of good friends and My smile of pride. Keep up the great work, My child!

Remember: Your good work will show up in all the friends you make.

Bible Treasure: *"Work hard so God can say to you, 'Well done.' Be a good workman, one who does not need to be ashamed when God examines your work. Know what his Word says and means." (2 Timothy 2:15 TLB)*

September 29

Hello, big brother or sister,

Did you know you have brothers and sisters all over the world? It's true! Because of Jesus, you're part of a big, fantastic family called the Christian family. You all share the same name, baptism, and promise of My love in your life.

Think about this: you have a brother in China, a sister in Africa, and many relatives in places like Japan and Mexico. Even though people might look different or speak another language, you're all connected through Me. When one nation struggles, it's like a family member in need—and family always helps the family.

Here's something fun you can do: pick a country from your globe each night and say a prayer for the people who live there. Imagine them as your brothers and sisters because they are! Soon, you'll see how big and wonderful your Christian family is. I love them all as much as I love you, My precious child.

Remember: Christians are all related through Jesus.

Bible Treasure: *"We who have been made holy by Jesus now have the same Father he has. That is why Jesus is not ashamed to call us his brothers." (Hebrews 2:11 TLB)*

September 30

Hello, My Sacred Heart!

Do you know what brings Me so much joy? It's when you and other Christians come together to worship and pray. Every time you do, I can't help but smile! I've filled each of you with My spiritual power and poured My holy love into your hearts, and seeing you united in worship fills Me with delight.

What makes Me happiest isn't just the songs you sing but the way you come together like one big, happy family. The next time you're in church, take a moment to look around. Watch people's faces as they sing—see how their eyes sparkle with joy, and their voices rise with love for Me. Each note you sing makes My heart burst with pride.

When you sing My name in your worship songs, I feel such great joy. Every voice is like a beautiful gift, and I treasure them all. Keep worshiping, My child, and know how proud I am of you and the love you bring to My family.

Remember: God rejoices when we worship together.

Bible Treasure: *"But they didn't want to. They were living for heaven. And now God is not ashamed to be called their God, for he has made a heavenly city for them." (Hebrews 11:16 TLB)*

"AND IF YOU w LIVE IN HONESTY TRUTH AS YOUR FATHER DAVID, ME, ALWAYS OBEYING IN ME. - 1 KINGS 9:4 TMB

HONESTY
KINGS 9:4

October 1

Hi, My honest child.

Let's talk about honesty—it's so important! When you're honest, you shine like a bright light to the people around you. Your family and friends will trust your words and actions because they'll see you always tell the truth and do what's right.

But trust can break when you tell fibs or do sneaky things, and it's hard to rebuild. People are always watching and listening to how you live. Did you know I send kind and honest people into your life to show you good examples? Your pastor, teachers, and friends can teach you what it means to live in truth.

And guess what? I love using *you* to be a shining example for others, too. When you're honest, it inspires people around you to do the same. Together, you can help each other live with integrity.

Honesty doesn't just make your life better; it spreads goodness to everyone near you. Let's keep sharing that, okay?

Remember: Honesty is the best way to live your life.

Bible Treasure: *And if you live in honesty and truth as your father David did, always obeying me.* (1 Kings 9:4 TLB)

October 2

Hello, My protector of truth,

I want to share something powerful with you: honesty always stands tall, no matter what. Being honest means choosing truth in every situation—even when it feels easier to tell a lie. Lies might seem like a quick fix, but they always tangle things up.

When you're honest, you're showing love and respect to others. People deserve the truth from you, and they deserve for you to speak honestly *about* them, too. Sometimes, standing up for the truth can feel challenging. Lies can be loud, but guess what? I'm right here to help you stay strong. Together, we can defend what's true.

Standing for truth doesn't just protect facts—it protects people. Imagine someone being blamed for something they didn't do. Wouldn't you want to step in and help? That's what being honest is all about—defending the truth and standing up for the innocent.

You're My warrior of truth, and I'm with you every step of the way. Let's always stand firm together.

Remember: Everyone must defend the truth to protect the innocent.

Bible Treasure: *"Be fearless in your stand for truth and honesty. And may God use you to defend the innocent,"* was *his final word to them.* (2 Chronicles 19:11 TLB)

October 3

Hello, My sincere child.

Let's talk about wisdom and honesty—two amazing gifts I want to grow in you. Did you know that I'll fill your heart and mind with wisdom as you practice honesty? It's true! I've given you many helpers: parents, teachers, pastors, and Church School leaders. They're all here to guide you and show you My ways.

But here's a secret—you also have something very special inside you: your heart and soul. I speak to you there, showing you the path of truth. Have you ever felt that little tug in your heart or that funny feeling in your stomach when something doesn't feel right? That's Me whispering to you to make the honest choice.

When you listen to your heart and use your mind to think carefully, you'll find the truth shining brightly. Connecting your thoughts and feelings helps you live honestly and love deeply. Trust Me—I'll always guide you in the right direction. Let's walk this path together!

Remember: You must use your mind and heart to be sincere.

Bible Treasure: *You deserve honesty from the heart; yes, utter sincerity and truthfulness. Oh, give me this wisdom.* (Psalm 51:6 TLB)

October 4

Hello, My Superhero.

Let's talk about something super important—being honest. I don't like it when My children cheat, lie, or deceive each other. That's not who you are! When you lie or cheat, you're pretending to be someone else, like a character in a story. But guess what? I made you to be excellent just as you are, so there's no need to make up a fake world.

It's okay to pretend when you're playing a fun game or using your imagination, but the truth is what matters when it comes to real life. If you tell the truth about what you've seen, heard, or done, you're living as the objective, honest you—and I love that!

When you choose honesty, you become a champion of truth. It's like wearing a superhero cape and standing for what's right. I delight in seeing My children live this way because it shines My love into the world. So be bold, honest, and the amazing, authentic you!

Remember: You don't have to pretend when you are honest.

Bible Treasure: *The Lord hates cheating and delights in honesty.* (Proverbs 11:1)

October 5

Hi, My Masterpiece,

Let's talk about truth and honesty—they're like best friends, always walking hand in hand. An honest person stands tall and protects the truth, but someone who lies? They're stuck making up stories that never quite fit together. It's sad when My children feel they need to lie—especially about who they are—because I created you to be wonderfully *you*.

When you hide the truth about yourself, it's like hiding Me too. And you don't have to do that! I'm a special part of your life, and I love when you share our relationship with others. When you tell your friends about Me, you show them what it means to have strong faith. You might even inspire them to grow closer to Me.

So be honest about who you are, My child. I've made you amazing, and there's nothing to hide! You're My masterpiece, and I'm so proud of how you shine My love into the world.

Remember: Always be truthful about your spiritual relationship with God.

Bible Treasure: *Lies will get any man into trouble, but honesty is its own defense.* (Proverbs 12:13 TLB)

October 6

Hello, My shining light of honesty.

People will trust you when you show them you're honest in everything you say and do. When you're honest, they don't have to wonder if you'll keep your promises—they'll *know* you will because you've done the right thing before, and they believe you'll do it again.

But trust doesn't happen instantly. Over time, you have to show people that you're someone they can believe in. Honesty isn't just about what you say, it's about who you are. It's hard for others to know what to expect if someone says one thing but does another. That's why honesty is so important—it's like building a bridge of trust between you and others.

And guess what? When you live honestly, you show the world that you follow Me and My teachings. Jesus taught His followers how to live honest, truthful lives. When you do the same, you're shining His light for everyone!

Remember: Honesty is a sign that you are a Christian.

Bible Treasure: *"By your honesty," he replied. "Make sure you collect no more taxes than the Roman government requires you to."* (Luke 3:13 TLB)

October 7

Hi, My Sacred Heart.

Did you know that what you do and say reflects on Me? When you follow My teachings from the Bible and listen to what you learn at church, you're showing the world that you're one of My precious children. Your good choices and kind actions are like a bright light, showing everyone how much you love Me.

I never want you to feel ashamed of what you do. If you make a mistake, don't worry—I'm always here to forgive you. Forgiveness is showing love, not because of what you've done, but because of who you are: My cherished child.

But remember, it's hard for others to see you as My child if your words and actions don't match what you believe. When you act with kindness, honesty, and love, you bring glory to Me and show the world the fantastic person I created you to be. You're a reflection of My heart, and I'm so proud of you.

Remember: It is difficult for people to believe you are a Christian if you don't act like one.

Bible Treasure: *For he could not judge and condemn me as a sinner if my dishonesty brought him glory by pointing up his honesty in contrast to my lies.* (Romans 3:7 TLB)

October 8

Hello, My loving child.

I want to talk to you about something very important—hate. Hate is not a good feeling, and it's not something I wish for you. Think of hate like a dangerous virus. If one person catches it, it can spread to others, and an entire community can soon be sick with it. But you can stop it! When you choose not to hate, you become like a shield that blocks the virus from spreading.

When you hear someone say they hate another person, be brave and speak up! Gently remind them that hate is harmful and doesn't make things better. Maybe you can even ask them to pray with you for the person they're upset with. Praying for someone softens hearts and lets My love shine through.

I love every person in the world and fill your heart with that same love. Will you help Me share it? Together, we can replace hate with kindness, understanding, and love.

Remember: God wants you to love people and never hate anyone.

Bible Treasure: *"Don't hate your brother. Rebuke anyone who sins; don't let him get away with it, or you will be equally guilty." (Leviticus 19:17 TLB)*

October 9

Hello, My friend maker,

I know it hurts when someone doesn't like you. Sometimes, you might feel like disliking them back. But I have a better idea! Instead of focusing on what's wrong, ask yourself, "Why does God love this person?" When you do, you'll start seeing the good things about them and find reasons to like them instead.

You know, I love *everyone*—no exceptions! Even the people you think are hard to love are precious to Me. Everyone deserves love, including those who don't like you right now. The best way to change their heart is to share My love with them. Be kind, reach out, and maybe even make a new friend. Who knows? You might discover you have more in common than you think.

When you show My love, enemies can turn into friends. And remember, that person who doesn't like you is one of My children too. Will you help Me show them what love looks like?

Remember: It is easy to turn an enemy into a friend by sharing God's love.

Bible Treasure: *"And now, O Lord, have mercy on me; see how I suffer at the hands of those who hate me. Lord, snatch me back from the jaws of death." (Psalm 9:13 TLB)*

October 10

Can you be a stop sign to hate, My child?!

I want you to know something important—not everyone who does bad things is evil. Sometimes, people make wrong choices because they're going through tough times or have been influenced by the wrong crowd. Maybe a kid at school feels pressured to act out because their friends are pushing them to do things they don't want to do. Deep down, they might still want to do what's right—they need someone like *you* to show them how.

You have the power to be a good influence, My child. If you see someone misbehaving or using unkind words, gently ask them to stop. Show them a better way by being kind, patient, and encouraging. You'd be surprised how much your example can inspire others! And who knows? The person you help might even become your new best friend. Together, you can discover ways to have fun while staying far away from bad choices.

I love seeing you spread goodness wherever you go. Will you help Me shine light in the lives of others?

Remember: Sometimes, you can change bad behavior by showing the person a better way to live.

Bible Treasure: *"The Lord loves those who hate evil; he protects the lives of his people and rescues them from the wicked." (Psalm 97:10 TLB)*

October 11

Hello, My truth spreader!

I want to share something significant with you—don't let hate take root in your heart, not even for bad things. You see, hate can start small, like hating a lie, but it can grow and spill over into hating the person who told it. That's not what I want for you. Instead of hating, I want you to pray. Pray for the things that upset you, and especially for the people who might be behind them.

When someone lies, it often leads to shame. Sooner or later, the truth emerges, and the liar feels embarrassed and hurt by their actions. My heart aches for them because I love all My children—even when they make mistakes. That's why I want you to help, not hate. Stand up for the truth with kindness and courage. If you can help a liar become a truth-teller, you'll bring us joy. And guess what? There's no room for hate when love is at work.

Will you help Me spread truth and love today?

Remember: Try to help people who lie rather than hate them.

Bible Treasure: *A good man hates lies; wicked men lie constantly and come to shame. (Proverbs 13:5 TLB)*

October 12

Are you ready for tomorrow, My child?!

My greatest joy is helping you choose what's right so you can have a beautiful life filled with friends, love, and happiness. Trust that I'm always by your side, guiding you to make good choices.

Have you ever felt a little twist in your stomach when you were about to do something wrong, like telling a lie? That's Me, whispering to your heart and reminding you of what's right. I work from inside of you, helping you shine My love and goodness in the world around you. And guess what? Other people notice when you choose to do good—they'll want to follow your example!

Your choices don't just affect today—they ripple into the future! When you live in kindness and truth, you'll teach others to do the same, including your children, someday. And their children will pass it on, spreading goodness for generations.

Remember: What you do today can affect tomorrow.

Bible Treasure: *"As for me, this is my promise to them," says the Lord: "My Holy Spirit shall not leave them, and they shall want the good and hate the wrong—they and their children and their children's children forever." (Isaiah 50:29 TLB)*

October 13

What is the most important thing in your life, My child?

Isn't it fun to have a little money to spend? Maybe you earned an allowance or got some for your birthday. What would you buy with it—a book, a toy, or perhaps a cool new outfit? It's exciting to treat yourself to something special.

Money can be helpful and do good things for you, but here's a warning: if you start wanting more, bigger, or better things all the time, money might try to take over your heart. Some of My children get so focused on earning money and buying stuff that they forget about Me. They spend all their time chasing after things, but those things can never fill their hearts the way My love can.

I want you to enjoy the gifts I've given you, including money, but don't let it become the most crucial thing in your life. Worship Me first, and I'll help you use what you have wisely—to bring joy, to help others, and to grow in love. Remember, I'm the greatest treasure you'll ever have.

Remember: Money can help you buy things, but it is not more important than God.

Bible Treasure: *"You cannot serve two masters: God and money. For you will hate one and love the other, or else the other way around." (Matthew 6:24 TLB)*

October 14

Hello, My Sacred Heart!

I want to teach you something powerful today about love and hate. Hate is a heavy burden. When you hold on to it, it weighs down your heart and makes you feel sad. But love? Love sets you free. It's like a light that shines and warms everyone around you.

If someone has done something to hurt you, it's easy to feel angry or upset. But holding onto hate only makes things worse. When you choose to love, amazing things can happen—your enemies can even become your friends! Love is stronger than hate; when you show kindness and forgiveness, you make the world around you better and brighter.

You don't have to wait for others to change their hearts. You can be the first to choose love and kindness. Will you share My love today, even with those who are hard to love? Together, we can make a difference.

Remember: You can be the first to stop the spread of hate; love everyone.

Bible Treasure: *"Listen, all of you. Love your enemies. Do good to those who hate you." (Luke 6:27 TLB)*

October 15

Hello, My hungry Child,

What's your favorite food? Is it pizza? Many of My children love pizza! It's delicious. But while pizza tastes fantastic, it's not the best food for your body. Foods like juicy fruits, colorful berries, crunchy vegetables, lean meats, and refreshing water are much better for helping you grow strong and healthy.

But did you know there's another part of you that needs feeding? It's your soul! Just like your body needs good food, your soul needs something nutritious. And guess what? The Bible is like a big, delicious feast for your soul. Every verse is packed with the good news of My love for you. When you read it, your heart feels happier, and your faith grows stronger and healthier—like your muscles do when you eat healthy food!

How about this: let's start with a favorite verse for your soul. Try memorizing Matthew 4:4; you'll always have soul food ready to go wherever you are.

Remember: You must feed your soul just like your body.

Bible Treasure: *But Jesus told him, "No! For the Scriptures tell us that bread won't feed men's souls: obedience to every word of God is what we need."* (Matthew 4:4 TLB)

October 16

Hello, My child. Did you read your Bible today?

Did you know reading and memorizing Scripture is like giving your soul a superpower? It helps you know Me better, and it even sharpens your mind! If you're curious about Me—and I know you are—your Bible is the perfect place to start. It's filled with incredible stories about how I've helped My children grow in faith and trust. And guess what? I can do the same for you today.

Here's something special: every Bible passage you read is My way of speaking directly to your heart. I want you to understand who I am and how much I love you. When you read My Word, you're connecting with Me in a way that millions of My children do, too. Isn't it amazing to know you're part of something so big and beautiful?

So keep reading this devotional, and don't forget your Bible! The more you read, the more you'll see My power at work in your life. I'm always here to help you, My child.

Remember: The Bible will help you learn about God and what God does.

Bible Treasure: *Jesus replied, "Your trouble is that you don't know the Scriptures and don't know the power of God."* (Mark 12:24 TLB)

October 17

Hello, Partner,

As you read the Bible, listen closely to what the Scriptures say—Me speaking to you! Each story and verse shows you how much I love and care for you and all My children. The more you read, the more you'll discover how I've blessed people throughout history. These stories hold the secrets of My power and love, waiting for you to uncover them. Isn't that exciting?

But let Me remind you of something important: I'm here to help you, not to do everything for you. For example, if you have a test, I can help you focus and remember what you've studied—but I won't give you an A if you didn't do your part. I'm your helper, not a genie in a bottle.

Ask Me for anything in your heart when you pray, and I will always answer. Sometimes, my answer will guide you in getting more involved in what you've requested. Together, we make a great team, My child. You do your part, and I'll do Mine!

Remember: God is here to help you, not to replace what you should do.

Bible Treasure: *Jesus replied, "The Scriptures also say, 'Do not put the Lord your God to a foolish test.'"* (Luke 4:12 TLB)

October 18

Hello, My Bible worm,

Understanding the Bible takes time, and that's okay! The Bible is like a treasure chest—you unlock its secrets gradually as you grow. As you get older and experience more, you'll see the beauty and wisdom in My Word in new ways. Some of My children, the Bible bookworms, read it cover to cover every year; each time, they learn something new and wonderful.

But you're never alone when you read My Word. I'm always here to help you understand it! The Bible is a spiritual book, and I will give you spiritual insight when you pray and ask Me for understanding. Sometimes, I'll send wise teachers into your life who can explain things to you and share their knowledge of My truths.

So don't give up! Even if you don't understand everything right away, keep reading. The wisdom and answers you're seeking might be waiting for you on the next page.

Remember: You will have to grow into the Bible to understand its meaning.

Bible Treasure: *Then he opened their minds to understand at last these many Scriptures!* (Luke 24:25 TLB)

October 19

Hello, My Bible Diver,

Do you know what makes the Bible so unique? It holds the answers to life's greatest mysteries—the ones people worldwide are searching for. Even teachers, pastors, and parents can only understand so much independently. But My Word? It offers wisdom beyond anything you can learn in school or from books.

I want you to know how precious you are to Me. The Bible shows you just how deep My love is and the fantastic things I have planned for those who follow Me. I don't keep your secrets—that's why the Bible is here, ready for you to read. The only mystery is the one you leave unopened if you don't dive into My Word.

Keep reading your Bible, My child. I'll help you grow in faith and understanding each time you do. Together, we'll uncover the wonders I've prepared just for you.

Remember: The Bible can show you things no one else can teach you.

Bible Treasure: *That is what is meant by the Scriptures which say that no mere man has ever seen, heard, or even imagined what wonderful things God has ready for those who love the Lord.* (1 Corinthians 2:9 TLB)

October 20

Who are you, My precious child?

Do you ever wonder who you are? Let Me tell you—you're one of My most fabulous creations! If you want to learn more about who you are and where you come from, open your Bible. The first pages tell how I made the entire world and created the very first human, Adam. He was the beginning of all people, which makes everyone on earth connect beautifully.

But there's more! Jesus brought something even greater than physical life—He gave you the gift of spiritual life. I am the Holy Spirit and live in every one of My children. Just like Adam was the first person to bring physical life, Jesus is the first to bring spiritual life to everyone who believes in Him.

That's why I call you My child, and everyone else is part of My big, wonderful family. No matter where you come from, my love connects us.

Remember: Even though we are born from different parents, we are all children of God.

Bible Treasure: *The Scriptures tell us that the first man, Adam, was given a natural, human body but Christ is more than that, for he was life-giving Spirit.* (1 Corinthians 15:45 TLB)

October 21

I see you, My Sacred Heart!

You don't have to do anything special to get My attention—I already see you and love you! You don't need to impress Me with cartwheels, handstands, or spinning in circles (though I enjoy watching you have fun). I see every jump rope skip, every bike ride, and every hopscotch game, and I'm proud of you. But listen closely—those things don't make Me love you more.

I love you simply because you're Mine. My love isn't something you earn; I freely give. Your faith in Jesus connects us; through Him, you'll always have My endless, unchanging love.

No matter what you do—or don't—I already love you more than you can imagine. My love for you isn't about how good you are at something. It's about how much you mean to Me.

Remember: God already loves you as much as possible.

Bible Treasure: *For it was through reading the Scripture that I came to realize that I could never find God's favor by trying— and failing—to obey the laws. I came to realize that acceptance with God comes by believing in Christ.* (Galatians 2:19 TLB)

October 22

Hello, My Holy child!

Do you know what "holy" means? Holy means something is extra special, set aside just for Me—to honor, worship, and learn about Me. Isn't that amazing? Last week, you discovered the Scriptures. The Scriptures are also called the *Holy* Bible. Why "Holy"? Because it's connected to Me! It teaches you My heart, inspires you, and helps you grow closer to Me.

Did you know the Bible discusses a holy day I created for you? At the very end of creation, I rested. I called that day holy—a day of peace, joy, and rest for My children. Some people call it the Sabbath. It's a special day for resting your body and refreshing your spirit.

I made the Sabbath so you could take a break from being busy and spend time with Me. On this holy day, rest your heart, recharge your soul, and learn more about My love for you.

Remember: *God made the Sabbath holy so you can find rest and know God.*

Bible Treasure: *"And God blessed the seventh day and declared it holy, because it was the day when he ceased this work of creation." (Genesis 2:3 TLB*

October 23

Hello, do you know My name?

Did you know that My name is holy? My name is unique and set apart to be used with love and respect. I don't want My name used carelessly or in ways that hurt others. When I spoke to Moses, I gave him My name, Yahweh, which means "I am who I am." Isn't that powerful? But don't worry—I have other names to help you call on Me quickly.

You can call Me "Spirit" because I am the Spirit of God who lives in your heart and soul. You can also pray to Me using the name Jesus. Every time you speak My name, remember it's a way to get close to Me and feel My love surrounding you.

Use My name joyfully, whether you're praying, singing, or just sharing your heart. My name is a treasure for you to cherish. I love it when you call on Me—I'm always here, listening to every word.

Remember: *Only use God's name for prayer and praise.*

Bible Treasure: *"Oh, sing to him you saints of his; give thanks to his holy name." (Psalm 30:4 TLB)*

October 24

Hello, My wonderful child! Do you know who I am?

I'm the Holy Spirit—the part of God living inside you! I fill you with spiritual power, creativity, and courage daily. When you feel inspired to do something amazing, that's Me working in you. Think of it as being *in spirit*—because when I'm with you, you can do things you never thought possible!

I helped Jesus, too. I gave Him strength, courage, and the ability to resist evil. And guess what? I can help you do the same things Jesus did! You can be kind to others, say kind words, and care for people who need help. Every time you choose to love, care, or create, you act just like Jesus—and I'm cheering you on.

So, remember, My child, you're never alone. Trust that I am always with you, guiding and inspiring you to be your best, just as I did for Jesus.

Remember: *In-spirit means God inspires you.*

Bible Treasure: *"Immediately the Holy Spirit urged Jesus into the desert. There, for forty days, alone except for desert animals, he was subjected to Satan's temptations to sin. And afterwards the angels came and cared for him." (Mark 1:12-13 TLB)*

October 25

Hello, My forever child!

Did you know I've given you the most fantastic gift? It's the gift of eternal life! Your mother gave you physical life when you were born, but I provide you with something even more special—a new spiritual birth. This means that while you live here on Earth in your physical body, you're also part of My world. You can feel My presence and know I'm always with you.

When you pray, talk to Me, or want to know more about Me by attending church or Sunday School, that's Me nudging your heart. I love it when you spend time with Me! I'm always working to inspire, guide, and help you draw closer to Me.

And here's something amazing: My gift doesn't stop with this life. When your time on Earth is over, you'll live with Me in My perfect home forever. Eternal life means being with Me always—starting now and lasting forever. Isn't that wonderful?

Remember: *The gift of eternal life comes from the Holy Spirit.*

Bible Treasure: *"Only the Holy Spirit gives eternal life. Those born only once, with physical birth, will never receive this gift. But now I have told you how to get this true spiritual life."* *(John 3:6 TLB)*

October 26

You received My promise!!

Did you know I've been keeping a very special promise since the beginning of time? I promised Abraham long ago that his family would grow into a great nation—and it did! But here's something even more amazing: that promise didn't stop with Abraham's children. It grew and reached people all over the world—including *you*!

This promise isn't about the family you were born into. It's about your faith in Me. When you believe in Me, My holy presence comes into your life, no matter where you live or who your parents are. And guess what? That makes you part of a HUGE, holy family! Every Christian is your brother, sister, mom, dad, or grandparent in Christ. Isn't that incredible?

You're connected to millions of people who love Me, just like you do. So celebrate, My child, because My promise to Abraham has been fulfilled in *your* life. You belong to a unique family, and I am always with you.

Remember: *God fulfilled the promise to Abraham in your life as well.*

Bible Treasure: *"Now God can bless the Gentiles, too, with this same blessing he promised to Abraham; and all of us as Christians can have the promised Holy Spirit through this faith." (Galatians 3:14 TLB)*

October 27

Hello, My baptized child!

Did you know that Jesus brought My greatest promise straight to you? He came to free all My children from sin and bring them closer to Me. When Jesus died on the cross, He carried the sins of the whole world—including yours—and made a way for you to be forgiven. When you tell Me your sins and ask for forgiveness in Jesus' name, I will ignore them.

But that's not all! Jesus showed you something very special through His baptism. When He was baptized, the Holy Spirit came to Him, just like I come to everyone baptized in faith. Baptism is a beautiful sign that you are part of My family, connected to the life of Jesus. It cleanses your soul and shows your faith in Me.

You are so loved, My precious one! I'm overjoyed that you're part of My holy family. You belong with Me, and I will always be with you.

Remember: *Your baptism and faith make you part of the family of God.*

Bible Treasure: *"We who have been made holy by Jesus, now have the same Father he has. That is why Jesus is not ashamed to call us his brothers and sisters." (Hebrews 2:11 TLB)*

October 28

Hello, My Sacred Heart

Did you know that in My eyes, you are perfect and holy? Yes, you! I know you don't always say or do the right things—sometimes, you might feel ashamed about your mistake. But don't worry! I love you so much that I'm always ready to forgive you. All you have to do is ask for forgiveness in the name of Jesus.

Even if you get in trouble or feel bad about what you've done, remember this: You are still My perfect and holy child. I ask that you keep trying your best to act with kindness and love, just like one of My children. Holy family members look out for each other, and you can show My passion by helping others whenever you can.

Why do I see you as perfect? Because Jesus died for your sins and the sins of the whole world! That's why you will always be part of My perfect Christian family. Never forget how deeply I love you, My fantastic child!

Remember: *We are perfect in God's sight because Jesus died for us.*

Bible Treasure: *"For by that one offering he made forever perfect in the sight of God all those whom he is making holy." (Hebrews 10:14 TLB)*

FRIENDSHIP IS RESERVED GOD WHO REVERED HIM: WHO REVERENCE

FRIENDSHIP WITH GOD

WITH THEM ALONE HE SHARES THE SECRETS OF THIS PROMISES.
PSALM 25:14 T.B

PROMISES.

PSALM 25:14

October 29

Hi there, My beloved friend!

It's Me, your forever friend. Did you know I gave you friends to help you grow and learn? Friends are unique gifts, people who will stick with you through thick and thin. They'll do fun things with you, cheer you on, and even help you see things about yourself that others might be too shy to say—like if you're talking a little too much or being too loud. A real friend tells the truth, even when it's difficult because they care about you.

And guess what? I'm your most excellent friend of all! I'll always tell you what you need to hear, not to hurt you but to help you. I'll be there when you're happy, sad, or want someone to listen. You can share your dreams, worries, victories—everything—with Me. Day or night, I'll never leave your side. You can count on Me, no matter what.

Treat Me like your best friend, My child, because I'll be with you forever. Let's grow closer every day!

Remember: God is your friend.

Bible Treasure: *"Friendship with God is reserved for those who reverence him. With them alone he shares the secrets of his promises."* (Psalm 25:14 TLB)

October 30

Are you looking for some good advice, My child?!

Let's talk about something really important: advice. Sometimes, it's easier to hear advice from your friends. Maybe a friend tells you, "Hey, that's not a good idea," you listen because they know you so well. Your parents and teachers also have great advice—they've seen and learned a lot—but I know it can feel easier to listen to a friend close to you.

Here's the secret: advice is a gift, no matter where it comes from! Your friends, family, and teachers all want the best for you, and they're there to help you make good choices. And guess what? I'm here for you, too. When you come to Me in prayer, I'll speak to your heart and soul with wisdom that will never steer you wrong. I'll always guide you because I love you deeply.

Remember the Bible—it's like a wise and trustworthy friend! The stories in it are full of people who faced challenges just like you. Please pay attention to what they learned, and let their experiences guide you, too.

Remember: The Bible is your friend that offers good advice.

Bible Treasure: *"The good man asks advice from friends; the wicked plunge ahead—and fall."* (Proverbs 12:26 TLB)

October 31

Hello, are you looking for joy, child?

Let's talk about something super important: forgiveness. If you want to keep your friends close, you must learn to forgive them like I forgive you. Everybody makes mistakes—it's part of being human! But mistakes are meant to stay in the past, where they can't hurt or embarrass anyone anymore.

Think about this: how many times have your friends forgiven you? Do they keep bringing up your old slip-ups? Probably not, because they love you. That's what forgiveness is all about—it's an act of love. When you truly love someone, you forgive them and let go of what happened. No more holding grudges or bringing it up later.

I forgive you daily, and I never remind you of your mistakes. I want you to learn to do the same. Let the past stay in the past so you can enjoy the joy and fun of today with your friends. The future is full of happiness when you focus on love, not mistakes.

Remember: Do not nag about your friend's past mistakes; find joy in their friendship today.

Bible Treasure: *"Love forgets mistakes; nagging about them parts the best of friends."* (Proverbs 17:9 TLB)

November 1

Hi there, My forever friend!

Isn't it amazing to have good friends in your life? Friends make everything fun—they play games with you, share laughs, and talk about everything you love. Maybe you and your friends cheer for the same sports team, watch the same TV shows, or even wear matching clothes to school. Who knows? They might even be reading this devotional just like you are!

And then there are best friends—those extra-special ones who feel like family. A best friend knows your secrets, laughs at your jokes, and gets excited about everything you love. Even when you're not together, they feel right there with you.

Guess what? I want to be your BFF—your Best Friend Forever! I'll always be closer to you than anyone else. I know everything about you—the good, the bad, and the silly—and I love you more than you can imagine. I'm always here, cheering you on, ready to listen, and walking with you every step of the way. Let's be best friends forever!

Remember: God is your friend forever.

Bible Treasure: *"There are 'friends' who pretend to be friends, but there is a friend who sticks closer than a brother."* (Proverbs 18:24 TLB)

November 2

Hello, are you friendly, My child?

Isn't it wonderful to have a circle of friends? These are the kids you laugh with, play games with, or chat with at school. Maybe you can even team up with them online for some epic gaming! Doesn't your heart light up when you unexpectedly run into a friend? It's like your whole day gets better just because they're there.

But I want to tell you something important: not everyone has a circle of friends like you. Some kids feel left out, maybe because they're shy or don't look or act like everyone else. These kids may not know how to join in or start a conversation. Would you try to be their friend, My child? I know it might feel awkward or even tricky at first, but they could become one of your best friends with a bit of kindness and patience.

Friendship isn't always easy, but it's worth the effort. Take a step of courage, reach out, and show them My love through your kindness. You'll make their day—and maybe even change their life.

Remember: Take time to get to know people; it is usually worth your effort.

Bible Treasure: *"If you are friendly only to your friends, how are you different from anyone else? Even the heathen do that."* (Matthew 5:47 TLB)

November 3

Hi there, have you shared Me today, My child?

Have you ever talked to your friends about Me? I hope you find time to share your faith with them. You probably already talk about your favorite games, shows, books, or sports. Talking about what you both love brings you closer together. It's fun to chat and text about your favorite things.

But you know what's even more special? Tell your friends about the beautiful things I'm doing in your life. Your friends might love hearing about how I'm helping you, and you can ask them what I'm doing in their lives, too. Here's an idea: what if you and a friend wrote a prayer together for Me? Imagine the three of us—united in love through that special prayer.

When you share Me with your friends, you talk about the most important part of your life. It brings us all closer together—Me, you, and your friends. That kind of connection is one of the greatest gifts you can give.

Remember: Sharing God with your friends may be the most important thing you will ever do.

Bible Treasure: *"But Jesus said no. 'Go home to your friends,' he told him, 'and tell them what wonderful things God has done for you; and how merciful he has been.'"* (Mark 5:19 TLB)

November 4

Hello, My holy child of God!

Did you know you're more than just My friend? You are one of My blessed children—a holy child of God! That makes you so unique to Me. But even though I'm your Creator and the One who holds everything together, please think of Me as your best friend, too.

I'm always with you, no matter what. When your friends aren't around, I'm beside you. I'll never stop listening if your friends get upset or misunderstand you. And when you feel lonely, I'll comfort your heart and remind you how much you're loved.

Isn't that what best friends do? I'm the one who sticks closer than anyone else. I'm with you in every moment, cheering you on, wiping your tears, and filling your heart with joy. You're never alone, My excellent friend—because I'm always here.

Remember: The Holy Spirit is with you even when your best friends are not around.

Bible Treasure: *"Now we rejoice in our wonderful new relationship with God—all because of what our Lord Jesus Christ has done in dying for our sins—making us friends of God."* (Romans 5:11 TLB)

November 5

Hello, My sweet, caring child!

Did you know you have a special gift? It's the gift of caring for others, and I gave it to you because I love you so much. From the beginning, someone cared for you—your parents worked hard to feed, hold, and keep you safe when you were a tiny baby. They did everything for you because they love you.

As people grow older, they sometimes need help too. Maybe your grandparents need extra care now—help getting around, standing up, or even eating their food. Do you know what's impressive? You can use your gift of caring to show love to them. Remember how they helped care for you when you were small? Now it's your turn to care for them with kindness and love.

When you take time to care for someone, you're showing them just how much they mean to you. That's why I care for you daily, My child—I want you to know how deeply I love you. Keep using your gift of caring to share love with others!

Remember: Caring for someone is a sign that you love them.

Bible Treasure: *"So Bathsheba went into the king's bedroom. He was an old, old man now, and Abishag was caring for him."* (1 Kings 1:15 TLB)

November 6

I care for you, My precious child!

Did you know that I care for you every single day? I'm the one who gives you the air you breathe and helps the crops and animals grow so you have food to eat. I'm the one who placed the sun in the sky to shine and bring warmth, and I send the rain to water the earth. Even the fantastic inventions you enjoy—cars, airplanes, TVs, and video games—came about because I inspired people to create them.

I'm not saying all this to brag, My child. I want you to know how much I love and care for you daily. Every good thing you have comes from Me because I want your life full of joy, blessings, and success.

I'm always here to protect you and keep you safe from harm. But to feel My care more deeply, pray to Me and listen to My voice in your heart. When you do, you'll see My blessings all around you—even in the little things!

Remember: God provides you with blessings every day; watch for them.

Bible Treasure: *"Jehovah himself is caring for you! He is your defender."* (Psalm 121:5 TLB)

November 7

Hello, My special helper!

Did you know that no matter what you grow up to do—whether you're a doctor, firefighter, hotel worker, or something else—you can always serve Me? In the Bible, you'll find stories of people from all backgrounds who became My special helpers. They cared for others, showed love, and helped My children grow stronger in their faith.

I have many jobs to fill, and you're perfect for one of the most important ones: caring for My children. It's not hard work, but it does take a loving heart. If you see someone lonely, be their friend. If someone is sad, cheer them up. And if someone wants to know more about Me, share your faith with them.

You might not realize it, but other servants of Mine have cared for you, too. Your parents, teachers, and others who love you are all part of My team, showing you how much I care. Now, it's your turn to pass on that love to others!

Remember: You serve God by caring for God's children.

Bible Treasure: *"But the Lord took me from caring for the flocks and told me, 'Go and prophesy to my people Israel.'"* (Amos 7:15 TLB)

November 8

Hello, My precious servant!

Did you know that we're coworkers? That's right—we work together to care for My children! Yesterday, I asked you to serve Me by helping others, and I want you to know you're never alone in this. I'm always busy watching over all My children, just like you'll do. I listen to their prayers and answer them in the best ways, even if it's not always what they expect.

When My children face tough times, I bring comfort to their hearts and send people like you to help. We're a team—you, Me, and others who love and serve. Together, we can bring joy and hope to My children, whether they're going through happy or difficult days.

Thank you for being one of My precious servants, My child. You make Me so proud! Caring for My little lambs is a big job, but with your help, we'll do amazing things.

Remember: When you serve God, you work with God to help people.

Bible Treasure: *"The Lord, their God, will save his people in that day, as a Shepherd caring for his sheep. They shall shine in his land as glittering jewels in a crown."* (Zechariah 9:16 TLB)

November 9

Hello, My amazing superhero!

A few days ago, I asked you to become one of My special servants to help care for My children. Yesterday, I reminded you that we work together as a team. Today, I want to share something even more exciting: every kind act you do for My children is like you're doing it for Me! That's because I live in every one of My children, just like I live in you. When you care for someone, you're also caring for Me.

Being My servant and sharing My love with others is a tremendous honor—it's more than a job, My child. It makes you a superhero in My eyes! But you don't need to fly or have super strength to be a hero. You're a superhero because you spread love and kindness to those who most need it.

Every time you help someone, encourage them or make them smile, you're doing My work. And I am so proud of you! Keep being My superhero, My child. You're making the world a better place every day.

Remember: A superhero shares God's love.

Bible Treasure: *"And said to them, 'Anyone who takes care of a little child like this is caring for me! And whoever cares for me is caring for God who sent me. Your care for others is the measure of your greatness.'"* (Luke 9:48 TLB)

November 10

Hello, My good listener!

Did you know your ability to care for others is a special gift from Me? I've asked you to be My servant and help care for the people I love with all My heart. To help you, I've given you unique talents and spiritual gifts to make you a fantastic caregiver.

The first step to caring is simple: *listen.* Everyone loves to feel heard; when you take time to listen, you show them they matter. Another powerful way to care is by showing kindness. Treating others with respect and compassion makes them feel valued and loved.

But the best gift you can give is your love. Spend time with people, listen to their stories, and show them how much they mean to you. When you do this, you're like a shepherd caring for a flock of sheep. You're not just helping them— you're showing them how I care for My children. Through your actions, they'll see My love and be inspired to share it.

Remember: When you care for people out of love, you show them how God also loves them.

Bible Treasure: *"Still others have a gift for caring for God's people as a shepherd does his sheep, leading and teaching them in the ways of God."* (Ephesians 4:11 TLB)

November 11

Hello, My Sacred Heart!

Do you know how much joy it brings Me when you're kind? You already know how to be kind—you've practiced more than you realize! Think about your pet if you have one. You know what makes your pet happy—puppies love walks, fetching sticks, and belly rubs, while kitties enjoy chasing strings, playing with balls, and curling up in your lap to purr.

You also know how to care for your toys and special things. You're careful to put your toys away so they don't get broken. You keep your favorite books safe from little siblings who might color on the pages or accidentally tear them. These small acts of kindness and care show how thoughtful you are!

Now think about this: the same way you care for your pets and toys, you can care for My people, too. Treat them with love, be gentle, and do your best to help them. Everything you've been given—pets, toys, family, and friends—comes as a gift from love. And when you share kindness, you're spreading that love to others.

Remember: You know how to care for your toys and pets; you can also care for God's people.

Bible Treasure: *"But we were as gentle among you as a mother feeding and caring for her own children."* (1 Thessalonians 2:7 TLB)

November 12

Hi, My fantastic fan!

What's the name of your favorite sports team? Do you love to cheer for them, tell your friends how awesome they are, and celebrate their wins? It feels great to share your excitement.

When you worship Me in church, it's kind of like that! Worship is a way of praising Me—showing your love and excitement for what I mean in your life. Many of the songs you sing in church are full of words that honor Me. Even the Bible has passages, like in Exodus, about praising Me.

Praise is simply saying or showing how much I mean to you. It's telling others how wonderful it is to have Me, the Holy Spirit, in your life. And guess what? I praise you, too! Every morning when you wake up, I shout joyfully to the heavens because it's another day I get to be with you. You're so special to Me, My child.

Remember: When we worship God, we give God our praise.

Bible Treasure: *"The Lord is my strength, my song, and my salvation. He is my God, and I will praise him. He is my father's God—I will exalt him."* (Exodus 15:2 TLB)

November 13

Do you need help, My precious child?

Did you know that many of My children praise Me because I help them when they're in trouble? Some of My children live in places where there isn't much food. They pray to Me for help, and I make sure they find food in their villages or send kind people from far away to share with them.

Other children live in places that aren't very safe. There might be wars or mean people trying to hurt or make them work for them. These children pray to Me for protection, and I stay close to them, watching over them.

What about you, My child? Do you need My help? I'm always here for you. No matter what's going on in your life, you can pray to Me anytime. I'll listen, and I'll help you in ways that are best for you. I love you so much, and I'm only a prayer away.

Remember: God can help you when there is trouble in your life.

Bible Treasure: *"God is alive! Praise him who is the great rock of protection."* (Psalm 18:46 YLB)

Hi, My happy child!

Do you remember the times I helped you when you were in trouble? When people feel grateful for the blessings I've given them, they often praise Me. Praising Me is simple—saying, "Thank you, God," or "Praise the Holy Spirit!" It's like a little celebration of what I've done in your life.

When you praise Me, it shows that you noticed My help or the blessings I sent your way. And let me tell you, when you take the time to thank Me, it makes My heart light up with joy! I smile a huge, gigantic grin because I know I made a difference for you. But guess what? I don't help you to get praise. I do it because I love you and want to see you happy.

You know what makes Me happiest? Seeing you share that joy by helping others. When you help someone and see their smile, it's like My greatest reward. Helping and spreading love is what brings real happiness!

Remember: God feels good when you are happy.

Bible Treasure: *"O my soul, why be so gloomy and discouraged? Trust in God! I shall again praise him for his wondrous help; he will make me smile again, for he is my God!"* (Psalm 43:5 TLB)

November 15

Hello, My joyful child!

What gets you super excited? Do you shout "Yippee!" and dance around when your favorite team scores? Maybe you and your friends cheer and sing together, celebrating the win. Isn't it fun to let all that happiness out? Those moments bring so much joy and make life extra special!

Do you feel just as excited when you get a good grade at school? You should—it's a big deal! Getting good grades takes hard work and focus. When you succeed, you deserve to celebrate, and I know your parents are proud of you, too. Take a moment to cheer yourself on for all your effort!

And guess what? I hope you're just as excited about my blessings in your life. When something good happens, take time to sing, shout, and give praise! I am so happy to see you celebrate the good things in your life. You bring Me joy every time you smile with excitement.

Remember: Always find ways to celebrate the good things in your life.

Bible Treasure: *"The man jumped up, took the stretcher, and pushed his way through the stunned onlookers! Then how they praised God. 'We've never seen anything like this before!' they all exclaimed."* (Mark 2:12 TLB)

November 16.

Hi, My thankful child!

Did you know people get super excited when they realize I'm doing remarkable things in their lives? Remember the first time you learned to ride your bike without training wheels? Remember how wobbly and scary it was at first? But then, you trusted your balance, pedaled hard, and off you went—riding down the sidewalk alone! I bet you shouted, "Look at me!" as you zoomed away. Wasn't that such a joyful moment?

Once, a woman had a bad back and couldn't stand up straight. She prayed for help, and Jesus healed her! Can you imagine how excited she was? She stood tall and immediately thanked Me for the amazing blessing.

I hope you'll always find things in your life to praise Me for, My child. Please start with the wonderful family and home I've given you. Every day, look around for little blessings— there are so many! When you see them, don't forget to say, "Thank You, God!" It makes My heart so happy to hear your praise.

Remember: You can find things to praise God for daily.

Bible Treasure: *"He touched her, and instantly she could stand straight. How she praised and thanked God!"* (Luke 13:13 TLB)

November 17

Hello, My hopeful child!

Did you know that many of My children come to Me daily, asking for things in prayer? Maybe they pray for a new toy, a good friend, or to win a big game. I love it when My children talk to Me and ask for help or blessings. But sometimes, they forget to thank me or answer their prayers after I help them. I understand—it's easy to forget to give thanks, even when someone does something kind for you.

One of My servants, Abraham, had incredible faith. Do you know what made him so special? He didn't wait until he received a blessing to thank Me—he praised Me even *before* he saw My gift! Abraham trusted that I would bring good things to him, so he shouted out loud praises and thanks with a joyful heart, even before anything happened.

I hope you'll have faith like Abraham, My child. Thank Me and praise Me before you even ask for something. Trust that I'm always working for your good; blessings are coming!

Remember: Thank God for your blessings even before you receive them.

Bible Treasure: *"But Abraham never doubted. He believed God, for his faith and trust grew ever stronger, and he praised God for this blessing even before it happened."* (Romans 4:20 TLB)

November 18

Hi, Is this a good time to talk?

Isn't it fun to find people who enjoy the same things you do? Maybe you have friends who cheer for your favorite sports team, and together, you shout and yell when your team scores. Or perhaps you're part of a book club where you can share your favorite parts of a story. You might even go to a car race one day and cheer on your favorite drivers as they zoom around the track. Exciting, right?

Being part of a church is like that, too! At church, you can join other Christians in singing songs of praise to Me. Worship is a time to celebrate together! You might hear someone talk about Me in a sermon, read something special about Me, or even say a heartfelt prayer. Church can be a joyful place where everyone is united in praising Me.

But guess what? You don't have to wait for church to give Me praise. You can sing, pray, or talk to Me anytime, anywhere. Whether you're alone or with others, I love hearing your voice.

Remember: You can praise God at any time or in any place.

Bible Treasure: *"And then all of us can praise the Lord together with one voice, giving glory to God, the Father of our Lord Jesus Christ."* (Romans 15:6 TLB)

November 19

Hello, My Sacred Heart!

Did you know that all the saints are constantly singing My praises in heaven? They sing the Spirit song because it feels natural and joyful in My presence. In heaven, there's no TV to watch, no video games to play, and no tablets to keep them distracted. Instead, they spend all their time with Me, and that fills their hearts with more happiness than you can imagine.

Being with Me brings so much joy that words of praise and songs of thanksgiving flow from their mouths all the time. It might be hard for you to understand now, but just being close to Me is all the saints in heaven need to feel complete and loved.

You can feel a little bit of that heavenly joy whenever you sing a song of praise or spend time with Me in prayer. Praise and prayer connect your heart to Mine, and I love every moment we share.

Remember: We are like the heavenly saints when we praise God.

Bible Treasure: *"After this I heard the shouting of a vast crowd in heaven, 'Hallelujah! Praise the Lord! Salvation is from our God. Honor and authority belong to him alone.'"* (Revelation 19:1 TLB)

November 20

What are you thankful for today, My precious child?

I want you to know something wonderful—I'm thankful for YOU! Whenever you talk to Me, whether in prayer, through a song, or just by thinking of Me, it fills My heart with joy. I love seeing the kindness you show others, especially out of love for Me. Did you know that when you help someone or share a smile, it's like giving Me a special gift? It makes Me so proud of you!

I'm thankful for our time together and every whisper of your heart that reaches me. I'm also grateful to your pastors and church family, who have helped you learn more about me. But most of all, I'm thankful for *you*, just as you are— right now, in this moment. You are My beloved child, and you bring Me so much joy.

Remember: God loves you and is thankful for you.

Bible Treasure: *"Go through his open gates with great thanksgiving; enter his courts with praise. Give thanks to him and bless his name."* (Psalm 100:4 TLB)

November 21

Giving thanks to Me is a wonderful part of worship, My dear child!

When you thank Me, it shows you've noticed the good gifts I sent you. Maybe it's a fun time with friends or a hug from someone who loves you. Perhaps you did great in a game or felt proud of your hard work on a school test. Guess what? I'm here, helping you, cheering you on, and providing everything you need.

Gratitude is like finding hidden treasures in your day—it helps you see how I care for you. Your parents, your home, the food on your plate, your clothes, your teachers, and the lessons they share are all gifts I've placed in your life. Keep your eyes open to notice them, and don't forget to say, "Thank You!"

And here's a secret: I'm thankful for YOU. I'm so glad I created you just the way you are. You're My precious child, and I delight in you every day.

Remember: Be thankful for what God does in your life. God is grateful for you.

Bible Treasure: *"I will worship you and offer you a sacrifice of thanksgiving."* (Psalm 116:17 LTB)

November 22

Hello, My blooming child.?

Even the dry, empty desert can bloom into a beautiful garden when I bless it. That's how powerful My love is! I take things that seem barren or broken, filling them with joy, gladness, and beauty. I do this with places and can do it with hearts, too—like yours!

When you feel sad, lonely, or like something is missing, remember I am with you, ready to make your heart bloom with happiness again. I fill your life with good things, just like I make flowers grow in the wilderness. I give you friends, family, and moments that make you smile. When you notice those blessings, sing a lovely song of thanksgiving to Me! Your joyful heart is one of My favorite things to hear.

So, trust Me to take care of you, no matter what. I'm always working to make things beautiful in your life, just as I promised.

Remember: Be thankful for God's blessings, and let joy fill your heart.

Bible Treasure: *"And the Lord will bless Israel again, and make her deserts blossom; her barren wilderness will become as beautiful as the Garden of Eden. Joy and gladness will be found there, thanksgiving and lovely songs."* (Isaiah 51:3 TLB)

November 23

Hello, My cheerful child.

Have you ever been at a party where everyone laughs, plays, and bursts with happiness? Joy spreads so quickly when people celebrate and give thanks. Think about a birthday party. Everyone is thankful for the person whose special day it is, and they celebrate with songs, gifts, and cake!

Now think about Christmas—the biggest birthday celebration of all! People worldwide give thanks for the birth of Jesus, My precious Son, who came to save everyone. On that day, joy fills homes, hearts, and even the whole earth. When people come together to remember and give thanks, their happiness shines.

Guess what? You don't have to wait for a party or a holiday to spread joy. Your smile is like a little spark of happiness that can brighten someone's day. When you share your smile, it's like passing My love to everyone around you.

Remember: Your smile can change your world.

Bible Treasure: *"The cities will be filled with joy and great thanksgiving, and I will multiply my people and make of them a great and honored nation."* (Jeremiah 30:19 TLB)

November 24

Did you make someone smile today, My child?

Sometimes, I give you more than you need—more joy, blessings, or even extra things like toys or snacks. And when that happens, I hope you'll let Me use some of what you have to help someone who doesn't have much. Sharing doesn't take away your happiness—it makes it grow! Imagine the smile on someone's face when you share and how it makes your heart feel even fuller.

Thankfulness works the same way. When you're grateful for what you have, it shines out of you. And when you share your blessings, it gives others a reason to thank Me, too! See how it keeps growing? I'm so thankful for you, My precious child. You are one of My greatest gifts, and I love sharing you with the people in your life who care about you.

Keep looking for reasons to be thankful, and I'll keep showing you new ways to share My love.

Remember: What you share gives another person a reason to give thanks.

Bible Treasure: *"Yes, God will give you much so that you can give away much, and when we take your gifts to those who need them they will break out into thanksgiving and praise to God for your help."* (2 Corinthians 9:11 TLB)

November 25

Being thankful grows deep roots, My child,?

Right now, your faith is just beginning to sprout. But don't worry—you have your whole life to grow stronger and closer to Me. Plants need deep roots to stay strong during storms, and you need deep roots of faith to handle the tough times in life. The more you grow, the more connected you'll be to Me, and nothing can shake you!

One of the best ways to grow is by learning more about Jesus. Did you know even He faced hard times? People made fun of Him for what He believed, and some places didn't welcome Him. But Jesus never gave up. His faith was like a tall tree with roots so profound nothing could knock it down. You can be like that too!

Read your Bible and discover how Jesus lived. The more you follow His example, the stronger your faith will become. And as your faith grows, so will your joy and thankfulness. You're just starting, but you're already on an incredible journey!

Remember: Faith is something you grow into; it only comes in your size.

Bible Treasure: *"Let your roots grow down into him and draw up nourishment from him. See that you go on growing in the Lord, and become strong and vigorous in the truth you were taught. Let your lives overflow with joy and thanksgiving for all he has done."* (Colossians 2:7 TLB)

November 26

Thank you for giving thanks to Me, My Sacred Heart!

Do you know how much I love hearing your words of gratitude? They make My heart so happy! But I want you always to remember something—I'm thankful for you too. I see the kind things you do to help others, and I celebrate how you're growing into one of My cherished followers.

When you're thankful for others, you're not just being polite—you're honoring the good things they do. And I want to honor *you* today, My wonderful child. Thank you for being exactly who you are. You make Me so proud with your kind heart and all the ways you live to honor Me.

Keep being a good and faithful servant, spreading kindness, love, and joy wherever you go. And know this: every time you do something good, I see it, and I'm thankful for you again.

Remember: God is very grateful for the good things you do.

Bible Treasure: *"'Amen!' they said. 'Blessing, and glory, and wisdom, and thanksgiving, and honor, and power, and might, be to our God forever and forever. Amen!'"* (Revelation 7:12 TLB)

November 27

Do you like to play Follow the Leader, My adventurous child?

It's such a fun game. You get to copy everything the leader does. But I want you to follow Me—not just for a game, but for your whole life. And guess what? Life with Me is full of joy and adventure!

When you follow Me, you'll find happiness in helping others. Have you noticed how someone's face lights up with gratitude when you lend a helping hand? That's one way to share My love. But here's something even more exciting— you can be a leader too!

You can show other children what it means to follow Me. Read Bible stories to your friends and talk about what you believe. Sing fun songs and dance with all your heart as you praise Me. Teach younger children how to pray so they'll always know how to talk to Me.

Being My servant and leading others to Me is such an honor. Thank you for showing My love to the world, My precious child!

Remember: You are a leader when you follow God and show other children what they should do.

Bible Treasure: *"Now if you will fear and worship the Lord, and listen to his commandments and not rebel against the Lord, and if both you and your king follow the Lord your God, then all will be well."* (1 Samuel 12:14 TLB)

November 28

Hello, My Spirit Servant.

I love you so much and want you to have the best life possible. I don't ask you to follow Me because I'm demanding—I ask because I care about you deeply. I know what's best for you, and I want to guide you every step of the way.

When you read your Bible, you'll discover all the wonderful things I've planned for you and the best ways to live your life. When you pray, it's like having a heart-to-heart talk with Me, and it keeps us close so you never feel lost. Going to church is another way to grow in your faith—you'll find friends who will help you follow Me, too!

And don't forget to be a Spirit Servant. Look for people who need a helping hand and show them love, just like I show you. When you love others like I do, your life will be joyful, and the people you help will be blessed, too.

Remember: God will lead you into the best life you can live.

Bible Treasure: *"Obey the laws of God and follow all his ways; keep each of his commands written in the law of Moses so that you will prosper in everything you do, wherever you turn."* (1 Kings 2:3 TLB)

November 29

Can you walk in My steps, My child?

Have you ever played the game of walking in someone's footprints in the snow, My curious child? It's so much fun! You have to match each step exactly, whether their footprints are close together or far apart. Sometimes, it's tricky, but that's what makes it exciting!

Now, I want you to imagine following My steps. Like in the snow, it can be challenging, but don't worry—I've given you everything you need to stay on the right path. Your Bible is like a map, showing how others have followed Me before you. Prayer is your chance to talk to Me and get My wisdom and guidance. And your Christian friends and family? They're there to walk alongside you and cheer you on!

The more you practice, the easier it will be to follow My footsteps. One day, you'll notice something amazing—it'll feel like my and your steps are the same. You'll walk so closely with Me that you won't even know where My steps end and yours begin.

Remember: You don't have to walk in God's shoes. You have to follow in His steps.

Bible Treasure: *"I have stayed in God's paths, following his steps. I have not turned aside."* (Job 23:11 TLB)

November 30

Following Me is a big adventure. Sometimes, it can seem difficult because you can't pick and choose which parts to follow. But here's the good news: the closer you walk with Me, the easier it will feel. When you practice following Me, it becomes a natural part of who you are.

Did you know the first Christians were called "Followers of the Way"? They got that name because they followed the way Jesus led them. Jesus even said, "I am the way, the truth, and the life." When you follow Me, you're doing what Jesus did, joining an incredible tradition that started with Him.

But there's more! As you follow Me, you become a guide for others. By the way, you live and love; you show people how to find Jesus and come closer to Me. You're not just following the way—you're helping others find it, too!

Remember: You are the way for other people to find Jesus.

Bible Treasure: *"But they delight in doing everything God wants them to, and day and night are always meditating on his laws and thinking about ways to follow him more closely."* (Psalm 1:2 TLB)

December 1

Did you know that following Me comes with many rewards, My joyful child?

I am thrilled you are one of my followers! You'll meet others who believe in Me just like you do, and together, you can worship, sing songs, and share your favorite Bible verses. Church can be a wonderful place to make new friends and grow your faith.

Sometimes, My followers gather at summer camps, where they learn about Me, swim, hike, play games, and enjoy the great outdoors. Doesn't that sound fun? Others go on mission trips to help needy people, showing My love to strangers who become friends.

Following Me isn't just about work. It is also about joy, laughter, and sharing special moments with others. I want you to enjoy life while you walk with Me. So, take the easy path of love and kindness, and let's have fun together as you grow in your faith.

Remember: Following God can be fun.

Bible Treasure: *"But fill the followers of God with joy. Let those who love your salvation exclaim, 'What a wonderful God he is!'"* (Psalm 70:4 TLB)

December 2

Hello, follow Me on the best path, My precious child.

There are rules and guidelines to help keep you safe and help everyone get along. You see them in school rules, game directions, or traffic laws. When people follow these rules, things go smoothly, and problems are avoided. So, please do your best to obey them and always do what's right.

But I want to guide you from the inside, too, with My love. I don't ask you to follow Me because of rules—I ask because I love you and want the best life for you. When you walk with Me, you avoid many of the troubles others face. Life won't be perfect, and challenges will still come, but staying close to Me makes the journey smoother and filled with peace.

Talk to Me daily in prayer, and I'll guide your heart. I'll lead you down paths paved with My love, where you'll feel safe, joyful, and cared for.

Remember: Let the Holy Spirit be your guide in life.

Bible Treasure: *"So now we can obey God's laws if we follow after the Holy pirit and no longer obey the old evil nature within us."* (Romans 8:4 TLB)

December 3

Hello, My humble Sacred Heart!

You have older, wiser people who are teaching you essential things to guide you through life. Listen to them and respect their advice—they've been where you are and learned a lot from their mistakes. They want to help you avoid some of those same missteps.

Mistakes are a part of life, and they help keep people humble. Nobody is perfect, and guess what? You don't have to be! Being humble means knowing when you need help and being willing to ask for it. That's a gift, not a weakness.

There will always be times when you need someone stronger, wiser, or more experienced to lend a hand. And just as others help you, there will be times when you can use your strengths to help someone else. That's how I designed My children—to support and care for one another.

Be humble, My child, and wise enough to ask for help when needed. I'm always here, and so are the wonderful people I've placed in your life.

Remember: God blesses those who know when to ask for help.

Bible Treasure: *"You younger men, follow the leadership of those who are older. And all of you serve each other with humble spirits, for God gives special blessings to those who are humble but sets himself against those who are proud."* (1 Peter 5:5 TLB)

December 4

Hi there, My turnaround child!

Do you know what it means to repent? It's not just a big word—it's a chance to turn back to Me when you've done something wrong. Repentance means saying, "I'm sorry," not just with your words but with your heart. It's about realizing you've gone off track and decided to follow Me again.

Sometimes, you might forget to walk in My ways. That's okay—it happens to all My children. But don't ever let guilt or fear keep you away from Me. When you come to Me and say, "I'm sorry," I'm right here to wrap you up in My love and tell you, "I forgive you."

No one is perfect, but I love you perfectly. Repentance isn't about feeling bad forever—it's about feeling free. It's your way of staying close to Me, no matter what. And guess what? My forgiveness is always ready for you.

Remember: Repentance is a way of saying you're sorry to God.

Bible Treasure: *When you turn back to Me, you'll be ready to help others find their way, too. "Then I will teach your ways to other sinners, and they—guilty like me—will repent and return to you." (Psalm 51:13 TLB)*

December 5

Hello, My Retentive Heart,

Do you know what sin is? Sin is anything that pulls you away from Me. It could be a lie, unkind words, or even forgetting to act like one of My followers. When you sin, I'm still here with you, listening to your prayers and loving you. But sin can make it harder for you to hear My voice or feel My presence, like a cloudy day hiding the sunshine.

Repentance is how you clear those clouds away! When you say, "I'm sorry," and mean it, your heart opens up to Me again. You'll start to hear My guidance and feel My love shining on you, just like before. Don't ever be afraid to come to Me and ask for forgiveness. I love you so much, and My forgiveness is always ready for you.

And remember, when you're in trouble, talk to your parents too—they love you deeply, just like I do, and they'll help you find your way.

Remember: Ask God to forgive your sins. God will always forgive you out of love.

Bible Treasure: *"The high and lofty One who inhabits eternity, the Holy One, says this: I live in that high and holy place where those with contrite, humble spirits dwell; and I refresh the humble and give new courage to those with repentant hearts." (Isaiah 57:15 TLB)*

December 6

Hello, My loved child!

Have you ever felt the quietness during church when everyone bows their heads to pray? That's a special time for you to talk to Me. In those moments, you can tell me about anything you've done or said, even though you know it wasn't right. Don't be scared or shy—everyone around you is doing the same thing, sharing their hearts with Me and asking for forgiveness.

You see, My child, no one is perfect. Like you, everyone in your church, family, and community has made mistakes. But here's the good news: I offer forgiveness to all My children. When you come to Me and say, "I'm sorry," I take your guilt away and replace it with love. Repentance isn't about feeling bad—it's about feeling free and loved as you walk closely with Me again.

Remember: God will love your sins away.

Bible Treasure: *"Let us examine ourselves instead, and let us repent and turn again to the Lord." (Lamentations 3:40 TLB)*

December 7

Hello, My baptized child!

Have you heard about John the Baptizer? He had an important message for everyone: "Repent and turn back to God!" John used water to baptize people, showing they wanted to clean their hearts and start fresh with Me. But he also told them this was just the beginning.

John talked about Jesus, who would bring more power and love to baptism. When Jesus came, He showed everyone how necessary baptism is by being baptized Himself. Isn't that incredible? When you were baptized, you followed in His footsteps! The water washed you clean on the outside, but something remarkable happened—I came to live in your heart and soul.

Through your baptism, you became part of My big family and received the promise of eternal life with Me. My Spirit is with you always, guiding you, loving you, and filling your heart with joy. Baptism isn't just a moment—it's the start of a lifelong journey with Me by your side.

Remember: The Holy Spirit is a gift of baptism.

Bible Treasure: *"With water I baptize those who repent of their sins; but someone else is coming, far greater than I am, so great that I am not worthy to carry his shoes! He shall baptize you with the Holy Spirit and with fire." (Matthew 3:11 TLB)*

December 8

Hello, My precious child, I am here!

Have you ever felt like you've made too many mistakes or done something so wrong that I couldn't still love you? Let Me tell you something beautiful—I will never stop loving you. Not for a second. Not even when you think you've wandered too far from Me.

I'm here for everyone, especially My children, who feel lost or need extra help. When you make mistakes, you can always come back to Me. All it takes is turning your heart toward Me and saying, "I'm sorry." When you do, you'll feel My love surrounding you, just like it always has.

I'm by your side in your happiest moments and when life feels hard. No matter what, My love for you never changes. Just call on Me, My wonderful child, and I'll always be here.

Remember: God will never abandon you.

Bible Treasure: *"When Jesus heard what they were saying, he told them, 'Sick people need the doctor, not healthy ones! I haven't come to tell good people to repent, but the bad ones.'"* *(Mark 2:17 TLB)*

December 9

Hello, did you hear angels singing, child?

Do you know what makes Me and all of heaven burst into song? It's when you pray to Me and say, "I'm sorry." When you repent, I forgive you with so much joy that I sing and dance, and even the angels join in! We celebrate because it shows Me that you're learning to walk the right path of love and goodness.

Repentance isn't just about admitting you've done something wrong; it's about wanting to make things right. When you come to Me, I don't scold or turn away. Instead, I open My arms and help you fix what went wrong. Repentance puts your heart back in tune with Mine, placing you on the best path for your life.

Never be afraid to tell Me when you've made a mistake. I'm here to forgive you, guide you, and celebrate the beautiful journey of your heart turning back to Me. You are so loved, My child!

Remember: The angels in heaven sing every time someone repents.

Bible Treasure: *"In the same way there is joy in the presence of the angels of God when one sinner repents." (Luke 15:10 TLB)*

December 10

Hello, My Sacred Heart!

Do you know what repentance means? It's not a punishment—it's a gift! Sometimes, you might feel guilty when you've done something wrong, but your heart tells you it's time to return to Me. And when you do, I'm ready to fill you with love and forgiveness.

Baptism is My unique way of showing you and all My children that My love never stops, even when you make mistakes. When you're baptized, something incredible happens—you receive Me as a gift. I am the Holy Spirit, and I live in your heart and soul, guiding you and helping you live a life full of love and goodness.

So, never be afraid to pray and turn away from doing wrong. I'm always here for you, ready to forgive and love you. You're My precious child, and I'll never stop caring for you.

Remember: You receive the gift of the Holy Spirit in baptism.

Bible Treasure: *"And Peter replied, 'Each one of you must turn from sin, return to God, and be baptized in the name of Jesus Christ for the forgiveness of your sins; then you also shall receive this gift, the Holy Spirit.'" (Acts 2:38 TLB)*

December 11

Do you know what it means to serve someone, My holy child? When you serve someone, you do things for them and help them with their job or whatever they do in life. There are many things you can serve in your lifetime, My young child. Some people spend their entire life helping the place they work. They become so wrapped up in what they do that t they forget about other people. Work becomes their life, and they are only interested in what happens at work.

I need your help in becoming My servant. I do not want you to become so wrapped up in serving Me that you forget about your friends or family. You can serve Me and still have fun with your friends. You can play with your friends because they are part. Of the people I want you to help Mem serve.

You must choose whom you will serve in life, My child. I hope you will decide to help Me and your friends and family.

Remember
You can still have fun and serve God.

But if you are unwilling to obey the Lord, then decide today whom you will obey. Will it be the **god**s of your ancestors beyond the Euphrates or the **god**s of the Amorites here in this land? But as for me and my family, we will **serve** the Lord." (Joshua 24:15 TLB)

December 12

There is a constructive way you can serve Me, My darling child. Pray for your friends and family members. When you think that your friends are having a difficult time, come to Me in prayer and ask Me to help them. If a member of your family did something great, say a prayer of thanksgiving to Me to celebrate their hachement.

Prayer is your best assistant in My service. When you serve Me, we form a partnership where we work together. You may pray to Me to help someone, but I may ask for your help in serving them.

Always remember that we work together to help all of My children. The work you do will give glory to Me.

Remember
The service you perform brings glory to God.

Sometimes I answer your prayer by asking you to become involved in the solution.

God knows how often I pray for you. Day and night I bring you and your needs in prayer to the one I **serve** with all my might, telling others the Good News about his Son. (Romans 1:19 TLB)

December 13

You do not have to pretend to be someone special when you become one of My servants, My glorious child. I asked for your help because of who you are and what you can do; you don't have to pretend to be special. You are special just the way you are. Just act naturally as if you were playing with your friends. I know how much you enjoy playing with your friends.

I want you to show your friends that they can serve Me just like you are serving Me. They don't have to change who they are or learn any special skills. All that you and your friends have to do is love each other just like I love you. When you love someone, it is easier for you to help them because you accept who they are.

I accept you and your friends for who you are out of, My love. Because I love you and accept you, you are My perfect choice to help serve My children.

Remember
God asked you to serve because you have a loving heart.

For we speak as messengers from **God**, trusted by him to tell the truth; we change his message not one bit to suit the taste of those who hear it; for we **serve God** alone, who examines our hearts' deepest thoughts. (1 Thessalonians 2:4 TLB)

December 14

It is not always easy to follow Me and serve My children. I gave you an example to follow to help make things a little easier for you, My child. Follow the life of Jesus, and you will always live a godly life. Living a holy life means you want to live as Jesus di and like I instruct you. Do you remember that the word "Holy" means set apart for My use?

You will also have heavenly helpers when you follow Jesus and serve My children and Me. I instructed the angels to help you whenever they can. Whenever you have difficult times, pray to Me for help, and I will have My heavenly angels come and serve you in your time of need.

It is an honor and a privilege to be one of My chosen servants, My child. I do not send you out alone.

Remember
The angels in heaven will assist you
in your earthly service.

It is quite true that the way to live a **god**ly life is not an easy matter. But the answer lies in Christ, who came to earth as a man, was proved spotless and pure in his Spirit, was **serve**d by angels, was preached among the nations, was accepted by men everywhere, and was received up again to his glory in heaven. (1 Timothy 3:16 TLB)

December 15

I ask you to serve My children and Me. I want to thank you for your service and dedication. I want you to know that I have a heavenly reward for you and all of My children who follow Jesus. I love all of My children so very much that I want them to continue being with Me forever. You will be united with Me in heaven with eternal life.

Eternal life is not so much a reward for your hard work but a glorious gift of My love for you.

My promise to you and My children is straightforward, and I will love you all forever. My love for you is so powerful that it will last forever. You and My other children will die one day; as your life on earth ends, your life in heaven with Me will begin. Don't worry, My child, you have a very long life ahead of you.

I just want to remind you of My promise to love you forever. Nothing in heaven or on earth will ever separate you from My love.

Remember
God will always love you.

But Christ, as a Minister in heaven, has been rewarded with a far more important work than those who **serve** under the old laws because the new agreement that he passes on to us from **God** contains far more wonderful promises. (Hebrews 8:6 TLB)

December 16

You do not serve a book of rules, My child. You serve Me, the Holy Spirit who loves you. Always remember how much I love you. Because I love you and all of My children, I asked you to help Me by serving My children in need. You must learn to follow Me with your heart and soul. I will talk directly to you in many ways, My child. I use the Bible to show the lives of other faithful Christians who followed Me in the past.

I use devotional books like this one to speak to you daily. I use your prayer time to listen and talk to you, so I know what you need in life. I also gave you the perfect life of Jesus to follow so he can show you how to live.

I live in you so that we will never be apart. I want to be with you every day of your life and lead you down the paths of My righteousness.

Remember
The Holy Spirit will instruct you on
the way you should live.

just think how much more surely the blood of Christ will transform our lives and hearts. His sacrifice frees us from the worry of having to obey the old rules and makes us want to **serve** the living **God**. For by the help of the eternal Holy Spirit, Christ willingly gave himself to **God** to die for our sins—he being perfect, without a single sin or fault. (Hebrews 9:14 TLB)

December 17

I hope you will take every opportunity to help Me care for My children. When you take time to help care for My children, you are serving Me. Never separate the idea that doing the people around you is different than serving Me. I am one with you and all the children of this earth. You cannot separate Me from you or My children what you do for one of My children you also do for Me.

I hope you understand this, My lovely child. It is essential because I want you to tell everyone else that you are all connected to Me. I live in the hearts and souls of everyone, so I am a part of everyone's life. So, you are helping serve Me when you assist someone else.

Serve My children and Me with an eager heart. Be as excited about serving Me as you are about playing a video game.

Remember
You are united with everyone through God.

Feed the flock of **God**; care for it willingly, not grudgingly; not for what you will get out of it but because you are eager to **serve** the Lord. (1 Peter 5:3 TLB)

December 18

I love your name, My lovely child!

I have something amazing to share with you. Did you know that the Father, the Son (that's Jesus), and I are all the same? Yep, we're called the Holy Trinity—three in one! It might sound tricky, but think of it this way: we're like one amazing God with three names.

Here's a terrific way to understand it: You are one person. But to your parents, you're their child. To your grandparents, you're their grandchild. To your friends, you're just YOU—their awesome buddy. One person, different names. That's how it works with me, Jesus, and God the Father.

Some things about us might seem puzzling right now, and that's okay! As you grow, I'll help you understand. For now, know this: I've been with you—and everything—since the beginning. I'll never leave you, no matter what.

Remember: The Holy Trinity is God the Father, Jesus, and the Holy Spirit.

Bible Treasure: "Before anything else existed, there was Christ, with God. He has always been alive and is himself God..." *(John 1:1-5 TLB)*

December 19

Hi, are you ready to spread some Christmas cheer?

Have you seen all those TV ads about Christmas? They talk about buying toys, cars, and decorations, but they forget what Christmas is really about—celebrating the birth of Jesus!

A long time ago, before Jesus was born, I sent prophets to share the exciting news that Jesus was coming. These prophets didn't have TV, phones, or email. They had to walk everywhere, talking to people face to face. But you know what? They did it! They spread My message to everyone who would listen.

Now it's your turn to be one of My messengers! Remind people that Christmas isn't just about gifts and glitter. It's about the greatest gift ever—Jesus. You can tell your friends, family, and even grown-ups why Christmas is so special. Trust me, even adults need a little reminder sometimes.

Remember: Christmas is a time to celebrate the birth of Jesus—the best gift I could ever give you.

Bible Treasure: "In the book written by the prophet Isaiah, God announced that he would send his Son to earth, and that a special messenger would arrive first to prepare the world for his coming." (*Mark 1:2 TLB*)

December 20

"Christmas is coming; Jesus will be here!"

Did you know I've helped people prepare for some of the most important events in history? A long time ago, I came to Elizabeth and Zacharias to prepare them for something amazing—the birth of their son, John. John's job was to tell everyone, "Jesus is coming!"

Now, I have a special job for you, too! Can you help prepare your family for Christmas? It's not just about decorating or opening presents. It's about celebrating the day Jesus was born! You can remind everyone of the real reason for the season. Don't worry—I'll be with you, just like I was with John.

All you have to say is, "Christmas is coming; Jesus will be here!" Simple, right? Like a little messenger, you'll spread joy and excitement about Jesus' birth. Trust me, your words will light up the hearts of everyone who hears them.

Remember: You are filled with the Holy Spirit to remind everyone Jesus is coming.

Bible Treasure: "But the angel said, 'Don't be afraid, Zacharias! For I have come to tell you that God has heard your prayer, and your wife, Elizabeth, will bear you a son! And you are to name him John...'" *(Luke 1:13-16 TLB)*

December 21

Hi, are you helping Jesus grow?

Can you imagine how little Mary felt when I sent an angel to tell her she would give birth to Jesus, the Son of God? She was young and probably a bit scared, but she trusted Me. Mary was chosen to bring Jesus into the world so everyone could see how much I love My precious children.

Now, I'm asking you to do something special too! You're responsible for caring for Jesus in your life. That means getting to know Him better every day. How? You can read your Bible, attend church, or watch videos and cartoons about Jesus. There are so many ways to learn about Him and feel His love!

And don't worry—you're not alone. I've sent lots of My children, like teachers, family, and friends, to help you grow in your faith. I'll guide you every step of the way. Together, we'll make sure Jesus grows strong in your heart.

Remember: You have to care for the growth of Jesus in your life.

Bible Treasure: "'Don't be frightened, Mary,' the angel told her, 'For God has decided to wonderfully bless you! Very soon now, you will become pregnant and have a baby boy, and you are to name him 'Jesus.'" *(Luke 1:30-32 TLB)*

December 22

Hi, I have a gift for you, My child!

Have you ever faced a problem that seemed impossible to solve? Mary felt that way, too. When I sent an angel to tell her she would have a baby who would be the Son of God, she wondered, "How could this happen?" The answer was simple: only by the power of God.

Do you remember what "holy" means? It means to be set apart for something special—something for God. I set aside Jesus as My holy representative on earth. He came to show everyone how much I love them and how their sins could be forgiven if they turn to Him.

Through Mary, I gave the world the greatest gift ever: Jesus. He came to teach, love, and guide you, My precious child. This Christmas, I hope you'll take time to celebrate My gift to you through Jesus. It's the most loving gift I've ever given, and it's just for you.

Remember: Jesus is God's loving gift to you.

Bible Treasure: "Mary asked the angel, 'But how can I have a baby? I am a virgin.' The angel replied, 'The Holy Spirit shall come upon you, and the power of God shall overshadow you; so the baby born to you will be utterly holy—the Son of God.'" *(Luke 1:34-35 TLB)*

December 23

Hi, have you decorated your heart, My child?

Have you ever been so excited you could hardly sit still? Maybe your birthday is just a few days away, and you can't stop thinking about the special gift you'll get. You imagine unwrapping it and playing with it all day, and it's so exciting you can barely sleep!

Now imagine how Elizabeth felt when she saw Mary carrying baby Jesus. Something amazing happened— Elizabeth's baby, John the Baptist, jumped for joy inside her tummy! Even before he was born, John knew Jesus was incredibly special. He couldn't wait for the world to meet Him!

The time is almost here to celebrate Jesus' birth! Like I was with John the Baptist, I'll be with you as you celebrate Christmas. Remember, it's not just about the decorations or gifts—it's about the joy in your heart as you celebrate Jesus, the greatest gift of all.

Remember: The celebration of Christmas begins in our hearts.

Bible Treasure: "At the sound of Mary's greeting, Elizabeth's child leaped within her, and she was filled with the Holy Spirit." *(Luke 1:41 TLB)*

December 24

Christmas is almost here, My excited child!

Can you believe it? Tomorrow is Christmas! The day you've been waiting for with so much excitement is almost here. But Christmas is more than just gifts and fun—it's about celebrating the greatest gift ever: Jesus.

Do you know what the name "Jesus" means? It means Savior. Jesus came into the world to bring forgiveness for your sins and the gift of salvation. Salvation means that when you mess up and do something wrong, I will forgive you if you come to Me with a sincere heart. It also means that you'll be with Me forever, even after you leave this world.

So tonight, as you lie in bed, let your heart be filled with joy. Sleep well, My precious child. We'll celebrate Jesus together tomorrow—the greatest gift of all time.

Remember: The name "Jesus" means "Salvation."

Bible Treasure: "As he lay awake considering this, he fell into a dream, and saw an angel standing beside him. 'Joseph, son of David,' the angel said, 'don't hesitate to take Mary as your wife! For the child within her has been conceived by the Holy Spirit. And she will have a Son, and you shall name him Jesus (meaning 'Savior'), for he will save his people from their sins.'" *(Matthew 1:20-22 TLB)*

December 25

Merry Christmas!

Jesus is born! But let me ask you—do you have room for Jesus in your house today? Maybe your Christmas tree is so big it takes up the whole room, or your decorations are everywhere. Maybe your home is packed with relatives, presents, and food. Could it feel too full for Jesus?

When Jesus was born, there was no room for Him either. Mary and Joseph had to stay in the part of the house where the animals lived. It wasn't neat or clean like your home—it was full of cows, goats, and straw. But even in that humble place, Jesus came into the world, and Mary lovingly wrapped Him in a blanket.

Today, as you unwrap presents to celebrate Jesus' birth, remember to make room for Him in your heart. You don't need a perfect space for Jesus—just an open heart. Even if your house is full of decorations and people, there's always room for Jesus with you.

Remember: You must make room in your life every day for Jesus.

Bible Treasure: "And while they were there, the time came for her baby to be born; and she gave birth to her first child, a son. She wrapped him in a blanket and laid him in a manger, because there was no room for them in the village inn." *(Luke 2:6-7 TLB)*

December 26

Hi, My Sacred Heart!

Did you know not everyone believes in Christmas? Some people have never heard the good news of Jesus' birth, and others choose not to believe. But on the first Christmas, I sent a heavenly choir to sing about the birth of the Savior.

The angels sang a glorious song over a quiet field where shepherds watched their sheep. At first, the shepherds were scared—they'd never seen anything like it! But the angels reassured them: "Don't be afraid. We're here to bring good news!" The sky was filled with music, and their hearts were filled with joy.

Now, I have a special job for you. Can you be one of My little angels? Share the good news of Christmas with your friends. Tell them how you celebrated Jesus' birth and how much joy it brings you. Don't worry—I'll be with you, helping you spread My love and peace.

Remember: Do not be afraid of the angel's song. It is good news for all people.

Bible Treasure: "That night some shepherds were in the fields outside the village, guarding their flocks of sheep. Suddenly an angel appeared among them, and the landscape shone bright with the glory of the Lord. They were badly frightened, but the angel reassured them." *(Luke 2:8-9 TLB)*

December 27

Hi, are you ready for our walk?

Do you know what the greatest present from the birth of Jesus is? It's the gift of walking with Me every single day of your life.

Before Jesus came, sin separated My children from Me. Sin was like heavy chains that kept them from being close to Me. But when Jesus was born, everything changed. He brought forgiveness, breaking those chains and opening the door for everyone to come to Me. Now, My blessed child, you can walk with Me, talk to Me, and have Me as part of your everyday life.

I hope you'll talk to Me often—anytime, anywhere. Whether you're happy, worried, or just want to share your day, I'm always here to listen. Nothing will ever stop Me from loving and wanting to be close to you.

Jesus made this beautiful life we share possible, so don't let anything get in the way. Let's enjoy every moment together!

Remember: You can walk with God and talk to God every day.

Bible Treasure: "For I am the Lord your God who brought you out of the land of Egypt, so that you would be slaves no longer; I have broken your chains so that you can walk with dignity." *(Leviticus 26:13 TLB)*

December 28

Hi, how do you feel, My precious child?

Have you ever been sick, My precious child? When you don't feel well, running and playing with your friends or enjoying your favorite activities is challenging. Sometimes, you only want to stay in bed, rest, and wait to feel better. Being sick isn't fun. You want to get better so you can be yourself again.

Sin is like a sickness, but it doesn't affect your body—it affects your soul. You might not feel it, but I do. Sin creates distance between us, making it harder for you to hear Me and follow My guidance. Your soul isn't as bright and healthy as it's meant to be.

But there's a cure for this sickness, and it's simple: forgiveness. When you've done something wrong, come to Me right away. Pray and ask for forgiveness, and I'll heal your soul. I'll make you feel new and strong again, ready to walk with Me daily.

Remember: Forgiveness heals your soul from sin.

Bible Treasure: "Only then, without the spots of sin to defile you, can you walk steadily forward to God without fear." *(Job 11:15 TLB)*

December 29

Hi, it's time for another walk, My child!

Do you like taking walks? Maybe you've walked through a park, along a trail, or even around your neighborhood. Walking is a great way to spend time with someone you love—talking, laughing, and exploring together.

Did you know I want to walk with you every single day? When you walk with Me, it doesn't mean just moving your feet. It means spending time with Me—talking to Me in prayer, listening to Me in your heart, and following My guidance in your choices. Walking with Me means we're always together, step by step, no matter where life takes you.

Some days, our walk will feel easy, like a stroll on a sunny path. On other days, the road may feel bumpy or hard to travel. But don't worry—I'll hold your hand and help you every step of the way. I'll never leave your side because I love you so much.

Remember: Walking with God is an excellent spiritual exercise.

Bible Treasure: "No, he has told you what he wants, and this is all it is: *to be fair, just, merciful, and to walk humbly with your God.* (Micah 6:8 TLB)

December 30

Hello, follow Me down the good path!

I'm here to guide you every step of the way. Sometimes, others might try to convince you to do something that doesn't feel right deep inside. That's Me, your Helper, whispering in your heart, "This isn't the way." Be brave enough to say no. It's always better to stand up for what's right than to follow along and find yourself in trouble. I want to keep you safe, far away from sin.

The best path—the one that leads right to Me—is full of joy and peace. You'll find it when you read My Word, spend time in church, and talk to Me in prayer. I'm always here to guide you toward the choices that will bless your life.

Sometimes, it's hard to stand up to your friends, but when you do, you might help them avoid making a big mistake, too. Saying no can be an act of love. Trust Me, I'll give you the courage you need.

Remember: You don't have to do bad things just because your friends are. Just tell them no.

Bible Treasure: *"Yet the Lord pleads with you still: Ask where the good road is, the godly paths you used to walk in, in the days of long ago. Travel there, and you will find rest for your souls. But you reply, 'No, that is not the road we want!'"* (Jeremiah 6:16 TLB)

December 31

Hello, you never walk alone, My Sacred Heart!

Sometimes, your friends might not understand when you talk about Me. They might make funny faces or even act confused if you mention reading your Bible, attending church, or praying to Me. Don't let that bother you. They're still learning, and I love them just as much as I love you!

When the time feels right, you can share a little about Me with them. Be gentle and kind—sometimes, your words can spark their curiosity. They might start wondering about the joy and peace they see in you. That's the beauty of good friendships! Friends often listen to each other and grow together. Who knows? You might be the reason your friend starts their journey of faith.

Thank you for spending time with Me every day. It makes My heart so happy! If your friend finds their faith, imagine all the wonderful things you'll get to share with them about My love.

Remember: Not everyone will believe what you believe; you can help them find their faith.

Bible Treasure: *"But we are children of God; that is why only those who have walked and talked with God will listen to us. Others won't. That is another way to know whether a message is really from God; for if it is, the world won't listen to it." (1 John 4:6 TLB)*

Bible Passages, Blessings, and Prayers

The Lord's Prayer (RSV)

Our Father,
who art in heaven,
hallowed be thy name;
thy kingdom come;
thy will be done
on earth as it is in heaven.
Give us this day our daily bread;
and forgive us our trespasses
as we forgive those who trespass against us;
and lead us not into temptation,
but deliver us from evil.
Amen.

Psalm 23 (RSV)

23 The Lord is my shepherd; I shall not want.

[2] He maketh me to lie down in green pastures: he leadeth me beside the still waters.

[3] He restoreth my soul: he leadeth me in the paths of righteousness for his name's sake.

[4] Yea, though I walk through the valley of the shadow of death, I will fear no evil: for thou art with me; thy rod and thy staff they comfort me.

[5] Thou preparest a table before me in the presence of mine enemies: thou anointest my head with oil; my cup runneth over.

[6] Surely goodness and mercy shall follow me all the days of my life: and I will dwell in the house of the Lord forever.

The Ten Commandments
(Exodus 20:3-17 TLB)

[3] "You may worship no other god than me.

[4] "You shall not make yourselves any idols: no images of animals, birds, or fish. [5] You must never bow or worship it in any way; for I, the Lord your God, am very possessive. I will not share your affection with any other god!

"And when I punish people for their sins, the punishment continues upon the children, grandchildren, and great-grandchildren of those who hate me; [6] but I lavish my love upon thousands of those who love me and obey my commandments.

[7] "You shall not use the name of Jehovah your God irreverently,[a] nor use it to swear to a falsehood. You will not escape punishment if you do.

[8] "Remember to observe the Sabbath as a holy day. [9] Six days a week are for your daily duties and your regular work, [10] but the seventh day is a day of Sabbath rest before the Lord your God. On that day you are to do no work of any kind, nor shall your son, daughter, or slaves—whether men or women—or your cattle or your house guests. [11] For in six days the Lord made the heaven, earth, and sea, and everything in them, and rested the seventh day; so he blessed the Sabbath day and set it aside for rest.[b]

[12] "Honor your father and mother, that you may have a long, good life in the land the Lord your God will give you.

[13] "You must not murder.

[14] "You must not commit adultery.

[15] "You must not steal.

[16] "You must not lie.

[17] "You must not be envious of your neighbor's house, or want to sleep with his wife, or want to own his slaves, oxen, donkeys, or anything else he has."

The Beatitudes
Matthew 5

"Blessed are the poor in spirit,
for theirs is the kingdom of heaven.

Blessed are they who mourn,
for they shall be comforted.

Blessed are the meek,
for they shall inherit the earth.

Blessed are they who hunger and thirst for righteousness,
for they shall be satisfied.

Blessed are the merciful,
for they shall obtain mercy.

Blessed are the pure of heart,
for they shall see God.

Blessed are the peacemakers,
for they shall be called children of God.

Blessed are they who are persecuted for the sake of righteousness,
for theirs is the kingdom of heaven."

Occasional Prayers

Table Graces

Monday

gracious and Loving Spirit,
We thank you for the food before us, which is
a testament to your abundant blessings.
Bless the hands that nurtured and prepared
it and the earth that gave it life.
May this meal strengthen our bodies,
filling us with energy and vitality.
May your Holy Spirit refresh our souls as we
eat, guiding us in love and gratitude.
Amen.

Tuesday

Spirit of Holiness,
You nourish me with food and water,
sustaining my body and soul.
You surround me with your boundless
love and overflowing grace.
You guide my heart to grow stronger in
faith, drawing closer to you each day.
From the first light of morning to the stillness
of night, your blessings fill my life.
With a heart full of gratitude, I give you thanks and praise.
Amen, Amen, and Amen.

Wednesday

Loving and Compassionate God,
Be present with me and my family as we gather
around this meal, sharing your blessings.
Pour your love upon everyone at this table and
bless those who labored to bring this food to us.
Guide us to care for your beautiful creation, keeping
the earth clean and healthy for generations.
Hold us close in your embrace throughout the day,
filling our hearts with your peace and guidance.
With gratitude overflowing, I give you thanks,
O God, for your boundless love and grace.
Amen.

Thursday

Gracious and Loving God,
With a heart full of gratitude, I thank you for the
gift of this food that nourishes and sustains me.
I thank you for my family, the source
of love and strength in my life.
I thank you for my friends, who bring joy
and companionship to my journey.
I thank you for the precious gift of life, each
moment a reflection of your grace.
Above all, I thank you, O God, for your unending
love, guidance, and presence in my life.
Amen.

Friday

Gracious and Loving God,
Thank you for the meal before us, a
gift of abundant blessings.
We are grateful for the love and care
poured into its preparation.
May this food nourish our bodies,
strengthening us for the days ahead.
May your everlasting love surround and sustain us,
Guiding us with grace throughout our lives.
Amen.

Saturday

Holy and Ever-Present Spirit,
Amid our busy days, we pause to
find rest in your presence.
Thank you for this meal. This is a reminder
of your provision and care.
Bless the food we share today, and may it
strengthen us for the journey ahead.
Bless the love that binds us, filling our
hearts with peace and gratitude.
Amen.

Sunday

Loving and Gracious Spirit,
Thank you for the gift of this meal
and the blessing of family.
May our time together be filled with
joy, laughter, and love.
Pour your peace over my parents, who
work so hard to provide for us.
Grant us all rest in your comforting embrace,
and may your presence renew our hearts.
Amen.

Prayers Before Bedtime

Monday

I place my head on this pillow,
Keep me safe all night long.
Keep all danger from me,
and all goodness beside me.
Let me rise with the morning sun,
Ready for another day of your creation.

Tuesday

God bless mommy and daddy.
Keep them safe all night long.
Rest their bodies and renew their minds.
Help them be ready for a new day,
Bless them for all that they do for me.

Wednesday

Give me rest tonight.
Please give me strength tomorrow.
Keep me safe every day.
Show me your love forever.
Amen

Thursday

Watch over me.
Rest beside me.
Support me from below.
Surround me with your love.
Keep me close throughout the night.
Amen

Friday

Please help me find peace tonight.
Keep my soul in your loving grace.
Rest me upon my slumber bed
let me rest in your heavenlylove.

Saturday

Give me rest this evening.
Be with me in worship tomorrow.
Bless me throughout the day.
Please guide me during my Sabbath rest.
Amen

Sunday

Give me happy dreams.
Wake me with a gentle smile.
Encourage me all day long.
Love me forever.
Amen

www.ingramcontent.com/pod-product-compliance
Lightning Source LLC
Chambersburg PA
CBHW020430130626
46549CB00001B/67